UNFORGETTABLE

My 10 Best Flights

Other Books
BY LANE WALLACE

Surviving Uncertainty:
Taking a Hero's Journey

Nose Up:
High-Angle-of-Attack and Thrust-Vectoring Research
at NASA Dryden, 1979–2001.

Flights of Discovery II:
60 Years of Flight Research at Dryden Flight Research Center

Wild Blue Wonders:
Exploring the Magic of Flight
  (Available through EAA)

Dreams, Hopes, Realities:
The Goddard Space Center's First Forty Years

Flights of Discovery:
Fifty Years at the NASA Dryden Flight Research Center

Airborne Trailblazer:
Two Decades with NASA Langley's 737 Flying Laboratory
  (Winner, Washington Edpress 1994 Silver Award
  for Excellence in Print.)

UNFORGETTABLE
My 10 Best Flights

LANE WALLACE

sporty's pilot shop

UNFORGETTABLE *My 10 Best Flights*
by Lane Wallace

Sporty's Pilot Shop
Clermont County/Sporty's Airport
2001 Sportys Drive
Batavia, Ohio 45103-9747

www.sportys.com

Published 2009 by Sporty's Pilot Shop

Printed in United States of America

Product Number: M265A

ISBN 978-0-9760676-4-1

Cover Photo courtesy of Cessna Aircraft Company
Cover design by Blaire Price
Book design and layout by Lori Wilson

FIRST PAPERBACK EDITION

10 9 8 7 6 5 4 3 2 1

To all the friends I've met along the way who made these flights both possible and memorable.

And to my Mom and Dad, who bought their little girl an astronaut outfit, even when girls couldn't be astronauts. If I grew up thinking the stars were reachable, it was because of you.

contents

prologue

It's said we have the ability to hold only seven items in the front of our conscious minds. More than that, and the brain starts to kick thoughts, memories, and facts back into long-term storage bins where they rest quietly, amidst many other thoughts, memories and facts until, or unless, something yanks them back out into the light.

The older we get, of course, the more crowded those storage bins get. Events, sharp and distinctive at the time, begin to blur and blend into a slightly fuzzy mass of memories known as "the past." In some cases, that's just as well. Some of our youthful behavior is best forgotten, or at least left buried under less embarrassing layers of history. But like it or not, the memory of most events and moments in our lives dim with time.

When I took my first flying lessons, each hour was clear and sharp in my memory. If you only have seven hours of flight time, you can hold the image of those hours easily in your short-term memory files. Twenty-three years of flying later, however, the flights are so numerous they're sometimes hard to isolate from each other. I've flown up and down the San Joaquin Valley of California so many times I can picture it in my sleep. Pulling one particular flight out from the pack, on the other hand, is a challenge. Was that moment I remember in 1996? Or '98? Was it en route to Chino? Or Modesto? Even the moments themselves fade, edged out of the easily accessible data banks by all the flights and moments since.

My entire aviation writing career, in fact, stems from my fear, only three years after getting my license, that I would soon lose the clear memory of the events that inspired me to become a pilot in the first place. My story about those events, penned one languid Saturday afternoon, caught the attention of my friend Jim, who encouraged me to apply for a job as an aviation newspaper writer. The rest, as they say, is history. History that, like a great New Year's Eve party moving toward midnight, gets increasingly crowded and hard to sort through.

And yet, it's not just one big blur. Even now, with thousands of flights behind me, there are some that stand out so clearly from the others that the memory remains sharply etched upon my mind's hard drive, impervious to time, distance, or any amount of additional data that's followed. In some cases, it's the details of the flight itself that make it so memorable. In others, it's the emotional context, or what the flight represented, that gives the memory its lasting power.

We all have those flights … where the adventure is so breathtaking, the air is so perfect, the company is so divine, the lessons so powerful, or a moment we stumble upon so side-splittingly funny, touching, or magical, that we know, even as it happens, that *this,* we will remember.

These are the flights we wrap up carefully and put away for the long, dark, winter nights of our lives, when we almost forget what joy feels like, or wonder how our precious energy and time has been spent. Gems we then unwrap, like Christmas morning surprises, so we can recall and relive all the laughter, learning, and life they contain, still sparkling like silver sunlight on a summer morning lake.

If we were to collect and line up a number of those moments and flights together, they also might create an illuminating montage of why we do this thing called flying in the first place. Of the laughter, beauty, power, magic, and learning that find us so clearly, sometimes, in the ever-changing and challenging classroom called the sky.

I write about flying for a living, which opens up opportunities for me that few pilots have the luck to experience. So some of my particular "top" memories are more unusual than most. But the reasons they stand out in my mind are no different than any pilot's best flights: because of their unforgettable beauty, companionship, emotion, adventure, sensation, learning, color, light, laughter or life. They are all, in the end, moments when I viscerally felt the gifts and joy of being alive … and wouldn't have traded that moment for all the money, fame, or accomplishments in the world.

CHAPTER ONE

Fifty-one weeks out of the year, Wittman Field in Oshkosh, Wisconsin, is an unremarkable, if scenic, stretch of open fields surrounding two long runways arranged in a kind of disconnected "T" configuration. There's a museum up the way, through the trees, where another small grass runway sits at an angle in between round-topped hangars that call to mind the days of barnstormers and signal fires; of Earhart, Lindbergh, Byrd and Post. But it's a quiet place, devoid of hustle, bustle, or grand, noisemaking events … as anyone who's been there in the long, snowy winter months can well attest.

During one short week of the year, however, all of that changes. For seven days at the end of July, the midwest airport of Oshkosh blooms into a golden city that acts as an irresistible magnet to pilots near and far, drawing us to return, like the swallows to Capistrano, at the appointed day and time each year. For Oshkosh (or the AirVenture convention at Oshkosh, as EAA likes to describe it) is the pilot's Mecca; the place to which all true believing fliers must journey at least once in their lifetime. And no matter how many times you return in the years that follow, no pilot forgets their first sight or encounter with the holy land.

I was lucky. Many pilots have their licenses for years before finding a way to get to Oshkosh. But due in large part to the fact that I was living in Louisville, Kentucky (so not that far from Wisconsin), my first pilgrimage to Oshkosh came just one year after getting my license, and only six months after buying my first airplane—a trusty but somewhat tired 1946 Cessna 120. I owned it in partnership with the man I was dating at the time; we struck a bargain that since he was an A&P mechanic, he owned (and was responsible for) the firewall forward, and I owned (and was responsible for) the firewall back.

The plane was a flyable project; mechanically sound, but cosmetically awful. It had a bare-metal fuselage that hadn't been polished in 20 years, which I thought was great ("Why doesn't everybody have a polished airplane? They're so pretty!") until I tried to polish it. The plane also had a truly horrific interior, with a dark brown, diamond-tuck Naugahyde headliner and side panels, and a crinkle-black spray-painted panel highlighted by a center panel covered in wood-grain Contact paper. And that's not even getting into the bright orange and green fluffy stuffing behind the Naugahyde.

Never having been to Oshkosh before, I fretted more than Jim did about what people would think. I looked with dismay at the stubbornly dull finish on the plane and that hideously awful Naugahyde interior we hadn't had the time or money to replace yet. *I* could see beyond all that to what she could be and would be with a little more time, love and attention. I knew how many smiles and moments she'd already given us, so she looked beautiful to me even without any shiny metal or paint. But how would anyone else see all that? To the unbiased, critical eyes of an outside observer she probably wouldn't look like much, and I cringed when I thought of her being criticized or rejected.

We had no illusions about having a Grand Champion airplane. And we'd taken her to other little fly-ins without worrying about her panel or polish job. But this was different. Flying your plane to Oshkosh is like bringing your spouse home to meet the family, and we wanted her to look her best.

Clearly, we couldn't get the whole plane spruced up before Oshkosh, but I remember working in the hangar every night until one or two in the morning the week before my first journey to the fly-in, scrambling madly to at least get the interior panel repainted and the annual completed in time to make the trip. I even stayed up an extra couple of hours that last night in a vain attempt to impose a polished shine on its oxidized metal skin. Eventually I gave up, resigned to whatever criticism or judgment the Oshkosh crowd might impose.

The year was 1987, back when the Oshkosh fly-in still had the big "opening weekend" schedule. We left Louisville after work on Friday and got as far as Joliet, Illinois … a town I knew principally from its role in the Robert Redford/ Paul Newman film *The Sting*. We overnighted there, fueled, and departed early the next morning. The mist was still clinging to the valleys and low spots as we climbed out and over a low-hanging cloud layer that the weather people had told us we would encounter en route. The layer was thin ... the ceiling below was about 700 feet, and the tops were only a couple of thousand feet high ... and we'd been told it was already clear well before our destination. But the feeling of detachment from the earth, above that puffy, isolated cloud layer, was remarkable.

The early morning sun lit the tops of the clouds with gold and silver highlights in the hazy summer sky ... bright enough that I wasn't even sure, at first, what that bright spot was that had caught my attention, a little bit ahead and east of us. But as we got a little closer, the bright spot came into focus as a beautifully fragile Curtiss JN-4 "Jenny," headed in the same direction and sailing along at the same altitude, just above the clouds.

We were a couple of hundred yards apart, but I still had the feeling that we were sneaking up on a skittish butterfly that might bolt if we moved too quickly. We slowed down to get closer to the Jenny's speed and shadowed it for quite some time. Normally, our 1946 Cessna was the oldest plane in the surrounding airspace. But in the Illinois sky that morning, it was as if we'd been transported back in a *Twilight Zone* episode to an even earlier time, where Jennies ruled the sky and *we* were the strange visitors from some future era—where metal had replaced fabric and someone had figured out how to build strength into thin, aluminum fuselage skins.

It's one of the best parts about flying an old airplane, far enough above the earth to leave obvious landmarks of the current day and year behind. Immersed in a timeless sky, in a plane from era long since past, time becomes a far more fluid element. Shadowing the Jenny that morning, it could easily have been 1946, 1922, or any date in between. I had the distinct impression of having journeyed out of time, to a place where perhaps, if the radio waves lined up just right, I might even hear a long-departed pilot's voice like a stray distant AM radio signal in the night.

Jim and I trailed the Jenny in almost reverent silence, not wanting to break the spell. And then, as if the crack between the eras was closing, the Jenny slowly descended from sight into the cloud deck below. One moment it was there; the next it was fading behind wispy tendrils of white vapor, and the next it was gone, slipping silently through a small hole in the clouds.

We remained quiet for quite a few minutes after that, somehow aware of having been granted a moment of grace akin to glimpsing a silver unicorn on a wooded, moonlit night. There are no more Jennies in the skies. We all know that. And yet, there it had been. Right there, in glorious formation with us, for a few magical moments in, or perhaps out of, time.

A few more miles down the road, the layer dissipated and we began to think about our approach into Oshkosh. The Wittman Regional Airport, during the EAA convention, is the busiest airport in the world; not something a novice pilot should attempt. The number of airplanes in close proximity is breathtaking, and multiple airplanes land at one time, on colored dots at various points down the runways. So if you can't spot land your airplane, don't bother applying. Given the number of airplanes converging on the airport at one time, the dedicated FAA volunteer controllers who work the show do a truly outstanding job of maintaining safety and order. Over the many years the show has been held, there have been very few arrival or departure incidents.

Being allowed in to the show, on the other hand, is another matter. Parking space at Wittman Airport during the show itself is first-come, first-served, and by the first big weekend back then, the airport was often already filled. Overflow planes had to park at other airports to the north and south … which meant you couldn't just pitch a tent next to the plane and walk to the rest of the show … or walk back home at the end of the night. Not nearly as much fun.

So getting a parking space at Wittman was a big deal. But many people arrive early to get spots, and here it was, already Saturday morning of the big opening weekend. From what I'd read about the show, our chances of getting a parking spot onsite were going to be slim. And as we neared the first call-in point on the approach, my worry increased. All the Cessnas, Mooneys and Barons calling in ahead of us were already being turned away from the overcrowded field. I was flying, and Jim was handling the radios. I asked him if we should divert. He smiled, shook his head, told me to keep going, and keyed the mike.

"Oshkosh approach, Cessna 66587 is over Ripon, inbound for landing at Wittman Field."

A crisp voice answered. "Aircraft calling, say type Cessna?"

Jim smiled, savoring the moment. "66587 is a *1946*

Cessna 120."

There wasn't even a pause. "Roger 587, proceed direct Fisk ..."

It took a moment for the words to sink in. Then I got a funny tight spot in my throat as I began to understand. Oshkosh wasn't the type of home where a disapproving aunt waited impatiently to judge your choice of mate. It was home for odd and old airplanes in the very best sense of the word. A place where no matter who or what you were, or how great your imperfections, you could always find acceptance and welcome.

At other airports, our little Cessna 120 had suffered the indignity of being shoved off a taxiway for an impatient King Air and neglected because we were buying only 12 gallons of avgas instead of 400 pounds of jet fuel. But not here. Here, the King Airs were told to go elsewhere, and the red carpet of welcome was being rolled out for a tired little tailwheel Cessna. With three words ... "Proceed direct Fisk ..." the controller had said it all. "No matter what the rest of the world thinks, little Cessna, you are special and valued and welcome here. Not *in spite of* your years and miles and patches and outdated electronics, but precisely *because* of them."

In that moment, I understood, without anyone ever telling me, the magic that is Oshkosh. And I was reminded of it over and over again, as I spent the next couple of days wandering among the rows upon rows of vintage and experimental airplanes lined up in the sweltering summer sun. I watched a woman polishing a wheel pant on her Lockheed 12A Electra, shunning shade and rest in a last-minute effort to give the plane its Sunday-best shine. I flipped though detailed restoration logs displayed proudly in front of pristine—and not-so-pristine—little taildraggers; took the time to read the details of engine and origin listed on countless other registration signs hung from windows and propellers. Out of the corner of my eye, I saw many of the owners furtively watching me, a tender and amusing study in practiced nonchalance and restraint.

I smiled, because I saw myself reflected so easily in their eyes. And I understood the unspoken plea that lay behind all the signs, photos, and mementos so carefully and meticulously displayed. "Please," they all begged of me, "appreciate my plane. Understand, somehow, how much love and care and sweat have gone into making it fly. See beyond the flaws in the paint; the patch on the wing, to how beautiful it really is inside. How many adventures it has unlocked with its wings. How many hours I poured into building her. See what it could be; how special it already is."

And I answered, because I understood so well how much the answer meant. "Nice plane," I'd remark. The eyes came to life with gratitude and relief. It didn't take much. A smile, a nod, a brief token of praise. "Yes," the words and gestures all said. "I see. I understand. It's beautiful, and special, and worth every dime."

Looking back on it, I think those moments are part of the tonic and cure that lure pilots to Oshkosh every year; inspire us to sacrifice sleep, run gauntlets of thunderstorms, and fight almost as hard to get here, sometimes, as the salmon running upstream. We make the effort because the Oshkosh gathering offers a sense of validation that we need; reassurance that we're not crazy and we're not alone. The rest of the year, we may find ourselves struggling to explain to friends and neighbors why we would buy a plane instead of a house, spend years of weekends covered in fiberglass instead of buying a ready-made aircraft, or why the plane, not the car, gets priority in the garage.

But not at Oshkosh. In this magical Brigadoon that emerges from the mist for only a few days every year, we are understood and welcome without having to explain a thing or say a word. No matter how bizarre our experimental design or how patched our antique, we know we can come home here, each July, and find acceptance among others who feel the same magic we do.

And although we may not be consciously aware of it, I think we also come to find that magic again ourselves.

Our attachment to flying is, after all, both a love affair and a marriage. For most of us, there was some unforgettable moment—a story told by an airline pilot uncle, perhaps, or the sight of a particular plane, or maybe even a magical evening flight—when we became entranced with this thing called flying. We fell in love, or we wouldn't have pursued it with such passion; devoted such time and effort and money to being around it. Like any new romance, it felt magical, full of energy, and we couldn't get enough of it.

But keep an affair going long enough, and the practicalities of day-to-day life start to creep in around the edges. We buy a plane, and suddenly there's the care and feeding of a new family member to worry about. The impractical little plane gives way to a bigger, more powerful traveling machine; improved avionics become tempting additions to the simple house we first owned. And while engine maintenance is about as romantic as taking out the garbage, they're both an indispensable part of any ongoing relationship.

Even Oshkosh recognizes the importance of these practical details. Armed with a shopping list and credit cards, pilots crowd vendor and manufacturer booths in the show's exhibit buildings. They also spend some time drooling over the imminently better-equipped and more practical new airplanes on display—their mere development cause for celebration because it means the aviation industry is still alive and kicking.

But relationships don't survive on practicality alone. And no matter how many times I've attended the AirVenture show, there always comes a point when I finally slow down, take a deep breath, and let myself wander away from the central display area. In search of some quieter surroundings, I find myself strolling through the show plane camping area. I stop and chat with a Piper Vagabond owner for a moment. His bare-bones panel lacks any electronics or advanced navigation aids, and a tiny, low-powered Vagabond would never fit anyone's definition of a practical airplane. But he doesn't seem to care. Indeed, there's a spark in this guy's eyes and grin that's utterly captivating—and entirely different than the measured look of satisfaction I've seen in the eyes of many pilots flying much more practical machines.

Move down to the ultralight area and this response is only magnified. I can't say I have any great personal desire to leave the ground in a lot of the contraptions I see there. But I find a smile creeping across my face as I watch three little helicopters dancing in amongst each other over the airstrip and hear the occasional "Yippee!" drifting down from pilots hanging out in the breeze overhead. Whatever else can be said about ultralights, one thing is clear. These folks are having entirely too much fun with these little machines.

It makes sense, of course. If a plane isn't going to be practical, it had better at least be fun. Nor is it surprising that the pilots who fly planes like Vagabonds or ultralights seem to have a more intense passion for flight; a spark and energy for simply being up in the sky. They have to, in order to choose machines with such limited practical appeal.

But it's contagious, this energy. As I wander among all the colors, shapes and beauty of these new and vintage planes, I start to feel a familiar and decidedly impractical feeling tugging at me inside, as if I'd accidentally caught the eye of a long-time lover and suddenly found my knees inexplicably going weak again. Without knowing exactly why, I find myself remembering all those wonderful summer evenings, before I knew anything about power settings or mag checks, piston pin plugs or speed kits. When all I knew was an intoxicating energy that somehow made me believe that flight could be magical and the sky could be mine.

This is the other reason so many of us are lured to this place every year; the drug that makes us burn the midnight oil, develop sudden, timely illnesses at work, and travel hundreds or thousands of miles just to get to a field in eastern Wisconsin. It's because among all these pilots who never settled down; these incurable romantics who value passion, fun and magic over anything practical, we find ourselves remembering why we fell in love in the first place.

The Oshkosh fly-in is a lot bigger these days than it used to be. Romantic that I am, I kind of miss the old set-up. But the heart is still there, tucked in among the trees and tents and multicolored wings. Whatever else has changed, Oshkosh is still a place where odd designs, impractical machines and even tired little taildraggers are special, valued and welcome—and where even the most practical and settled of pilots can recapture a little of the romance that made the marriage worth pursuing.

South of the Border
CHAPTER TWO

Everyone should fly to Mexico at least once in their flying career.

My own dreams of flying to Mexico started only a few years after getting my license, when I met a wonderful pilot from the golden era of air mail pilots and barnstormers. His name was Mark Walker, and he was an old man by the time I met him, in the late 1980s. He'd met Ernest Hemingway, and he'd forgotten more adventures in biplanes than I'd ever had. But he was still full of life, energy, laughter and stories. Oh my, was he full of stories! But the tale I loved best was the one about flying to Mexico.

Mark lived in Orange County, California, back in the late 1940s and flew out of the Martin brothers' FBO there. And he told me how he used to take an old Fairchild PT-19 military trainer, put a bottle of whiskey, a blanket, and a couple of steaks in the baggage compartment, and take a lady friend with him down to the beaches of Baja Mexico for the night. They'd build a fire on the beach, grill the steaks, drink the whiskey, and sleep on the blanket under the stars, flying back the next day.

I was entranced. Short of landing a flying boat in a South Pacific lagoon for a similar kind of barbecue, it was hard to imagine a more perfect combination of beauty and adventure. But it had gotten a lot tougher in the years since to just land on a beach in Baja and spend the night, and most of the pilots I knew weren't up for the vagaries of Mexican flying, even to established airports. So my dreams of flying to Mexico remained just that: dreams.

Ten years later, however, I had my own airplane and was living back in southern California again. I'd also found out that the gray whales I'd seen off the coast of California actually gave birth in a couple of protected bays on the Pacific coast of Baja, and that people were allowed to go out in small, outboard Panga boats among the mother-baby pairs in the bay.

Unfortunately, my airplane (a Grumman Cheetah with a notoriously weak nosewheel) was a far cry from a PT-19, or even a Piper Super Cub or other appropriate beach-landing aircraft. So that part was probably out. But flying to Mexico to see the whales still rang with the sound of adventure. I decided to go, and I enthusiastically began telling friends about my plan.

Their response was, shall we say, a bit more muted.

"You want to take your Cheetah WHERE?"

"Baja. I want to see the whales."

"Do you not LIKE your plane?" the common response went, followed by a whole list of horrors I was about to encounter. Mexican Federales with M-16s who would confiscate my airplane. Bandits who would steal it. Corrupt officials who would take all my money. Rocks on unimproved runways that would destroy my paint, gear, and prop. U.S. Customs agents who would take apart or confiscate anything that was left.

But I was determined. I'd been dreaming of flying to Mexico for 10 years, and it seemed an adventure worth undertaking a few hassles or risks in order to experience. Besides. I wasn't convinced all the horror stories were true. The Baja Bush Pilots association has something like 1,200 members. If flying in Baja were such a nightmare, that many people wouldn't do it on a regular basis. And those who had been there told of wide open skies, pristine white beaches, clear blue waters, and the best fish and shrimp tacos this side of heaven.

In any event, there was only one way to find out what it was really like, and that was to go there. So I researched everything I could about paperwork and procedures, convinced a pilot friend to come along on the adventure as a little extra security blanket, and finally got a good enough break in the weather to head south.

My plan was to clear customs at San Felipe, on the east coast of the peninsula, then head down to Guerrero Negro on the Pacific side (named after a ship that sank off the point there) to see the whales. After that, I planned to head back across to a town called Mulege on the east coast of Baja. Mulege is a popular destination with pilots because its Hotel Serenidad has its own dirt runway, which makes it a convenient stop. It also, for the record, has legendary margaritas that are so potent they should be placarded, especially after a long day of flying.

I intended to depart Southern California in the morning, stop at San Felipe and continue on to Guerrero Negro the first day. But a stubborn marine layer persisted until almost 3:00 in the afternoon, which meant we would be lucky to make it to San Felipe. No VFR night flying is allowed in Mexico, and all the controlled airports close at 5:00 p.m. And as I soon learned, when they say 5:00, they mean 5:00. Not 5:01.

As we crossed over the border, flight service wished us a good flight and terminated our flight following. There would be no more hand-holding until we were back in the States. We had entered the frontier land and skies of Baja, where one of the first rules pilots learn is self-reliance. You can fly almost anywhere you want there, but there is no weather service and little in the way of radar, communications, or maintenance services. Smart visitors to Baja bring their own tools and a large bag of resourcefulness, prudent common sense and flexibility.

As the minutes and miles passed, I began to get concerned. My GPS was predicting that we would arrive at San Felipe at 5:05 p.m. I bumped up the throttle. 5:03. I bumped it up some more. 5:02. By the time I got an estimated arrival time before 5:00 p.m., I had the throttle just below redline.

I called the San Felipe tower at 4:15 in my most charming voice, reported an optimistic 40 minutes out and asked if I could proceed to the field. By 4:30 we would be committed, because we wouldn't be able to make it back to any other

Mexican controlled field before closing time. I hoped a large dose of charm and advance notice might buy me a few extra minutes. The tower approved me to proceed, reminding me that the airport closed at 5:00. By 4:30, they were calling every 10 minutes asking for position reports. By 4:50, I had the plane in a full-power descent, wishing I could pedal faster to gain a few extra knots. I called my entry to downwind a good five miles out, putting on my landing light in the hopes that if they saw me, they'd believe I was in the pattern already. I looked at my watch. This was going to be close. When I got abeam the tower on downwind, my groundspeed was 143 knots and it was 4:59 p.m.

"Niner-four-uniform, it is 4:59," the tower reported sternly, as if I needed reminding. "You are cleared to land ... IF you can make a short approach." I cut the power, turned toward the runway, landed, braked hard, pulled off the runway and looked at my watch. It was 4:59:59. Not the ideal way to start my relationship with the Mexican airport officials, but another lesson I learned about flying in Mexico is that a courteous, charming, and respectful attitude goes a very long way. It's their country, it has a long and dignified history, the officials are very proud of whatever position they hold, and they want a little respect for all of the above. Go to Baja with an ego or attitude and they will serve it to you for lunch, along with a bunch of hassles and fines, and backed up with an M-16 or two. (A note to the wise: Don't argue with an M-16. Even if the soldier holding it is younger than your son. You will not win.) But show courtesy and respect, and they may even forgive you for landing at 4:59 p.m.

The next day, we left San Felipe to go see the whales, and I soon learned two more of the basic rules of flying in Baja. The Baja coastline is stunningly beautiful, but the land is unbelievably desolate and rough, and airports are few and far between. As a result, your primary instrument in Baja is your fuel gauge—especially because not all the airports have fuel, and even those that do can't always be counted on to have it all the time.

The consequences of landing short for fuel starvation or any other reason also figured prominently in my thoughts, because Baja is not a land where you'd want to have to put an airplane down. Find yourself with even an open cowling latch in flight (as I did on one leg) and you start evaluating all that those beautiful, remote, craggy canyons underneath you in an entirely new light.

"Flying down here, even a small problem is a big problem," a Cessna 180 pilot at Mulege told me as he stuffed his blown tail wheel inner tube with sand and rags so he could take off again. Indeed. It's a reminder to think twice before you attempt that difficult crosswind landing on that deteriorating runway, because fixing an airplane in Baja is no small task.

The good news is that because there is so little in terms of official assistance in Baja, the pilots who fly there are wonderful at assisting each other, whether it's loaning tools, parts or gas cans, offering advice, or sharing information. Pilots in Baja use 122.75 as something of a party line, calling to see if anyone in the vicinity of Guerrero Negro knows what the weather's like there, or if anyone's found fuel at San Felipe, or what the runway conditions at San Ignacio are like that day.

That party line can also, at times, provide some really great in-flight entertainment. On our flight from Guerrero Negro to Mulege, my friend and I were listening to the air-to-air frequency when an airline captain—I'll call him Dick—called in from 35,000 feet, asking if anyone was flying over Baja that day. A pilot from the same airline—I'll call him Wally—answered on the frequency, saying he was in a Piper, bound for the same hotel in Mulege as we were. The two airline pilots quickly figured out that they actually knew each other. Then came the $64,000 question.

"Hey, Wally," Dick asked, "is Nancy with you?"

There was silence on the frequency.

"Uh ... Wally? Your radio working?" came Dick's perplexed voice.

"Yeah ... yeah, it's working," Wally answered uncomfortably.

"So, is Nancy with you, or are you alone?"

There was another uncomfortable silence. Finally, Wally came on the frequency.

"Uh, Dick," he said, "switch over to 123.45, would you?"

I looked over at the friend who was flying with me. He was already reaching for the radio knob—along with every other pilot who was flying over Baja that day. This sounded just too good to miss. We came up on 123.45 just as Dick checked in again.

"So, Wally, what's the deal? Are you alone?"

"Uh, no," Wally stammered.

"Who's with you?"

"A friend."

There was a moment of silence. I could almost hear the

snickers filling airplane cockpits all across the peninsula. Then Dick's knowing voice came back on the frequency.

"What's her name, Wally?"

Silence. Then, reluctantly, "Tammy."

The snickers turned to out-and-out laughter, at least in my airplane. I could picture Dick shaking his head up there at 35,000 feet. "You be careful, Wally," he said before signing off.

I was still chuckling when I landed in Mulege an hour or so later, tied the airplane down and made my way to the hotel pool, where a number of newly arrived pilots had gathered. We began introductions. And when one pilot introduced himself as Wally, I couldn't resist. I looked at the buxom bleached blonde in six-inch heels next to him, smiled, and said, "Oh! You must be Tammy!" Everyone burst out laughing as I thanked Wally for the best in-flight entertainment I'd had in a long time.

Tammy sure was something. Two days later, when most of us had planned to leave, the single telephone line and satellite weather channel at the remote hotel showed that one of the worst winter storms to hit southern California in years was sweeping across San Diego with surface winds above 80 mph and icing, in the northern New Mexico and Arizona regions, from the surface to well over 20,000 feet. At Mulege, the wind was calm, the sky was clear, and the temperature was a balmy 80-something degrees. We were fine where we were. We just ... darn the bad luck ... couldn't leave.

That conclusion did not sit well with Miss Tammy. We were all sitting around figuring out Plan B, when she stood up in a huff, hands on her hips, and announced, "Well, I don't know about the rest of you, but I HAVE to leave. I HAVE to be back at work tomorrow!" She glared down at the hapless Wally, who averted his eyes and started squirming in his seat. There was an uncomfortable silence in the group. Domestic squabbles never play well in public. Finally, I spoke up.

"Honey ... you've never *been* shit-scared in an airplane, have you?" I asked her. A couple of the pilots started to chuckle. Tammy turned and glared at me, but didn't answer. "Because if you had," I continued, "you'd know that there's *nowhere* you have to be that badly."

An hour later, I walked outside and saw Wally untying his Piper. Another pilot from the group was walking back from the plane, shaking his head.

"He's *going*???" I asked incredulously, as the pilot approached. He nodded and shrugged, a look of resignation on his face as he turned and we both watched Wally climb on board and fire up the engines.

"I told him I didn't care how good she was, it wasn't worth dying for," the pilot said straight-faced, still looking out toward Wally's plane. Finally he sighed, shrugged again, and turned to walk back to the pool. "But what're you gonna do?"

I have no idea how Wally's flight turned out. As for myself, I ended up having to spend two more days swimming in the crystal clear waters of the Bay of California, sipping margaritas by the hotel pool, and exploring some of the many white sand beaches in the area.

One night, my friend and I went to an unadvertised local restaurant perched on the edge of a sandy beach where the river met the sea. They didn't speak any English there, and I spoke almost no Spanish. But when the owner couldn't find us a clean table inside, he motioned for us to wait a minute. A table, tablecloth, two chairs and a hurricane candle lamp were whisked outside to the beach right in front of the restaurant. The owner gestured for us to sit. Margaritas and fresh shrimp and fish dishes in various types of sauces and tortillas arrived in front of us. A full moon was rising to the east, casting a bright silver moonbeam across the water, straight toward our table, where the water was lapping softly at the sand only a few yards away. Music and voices filtered out into the night from the brightly lit tavern behind us.

It wasn't a PT-19. And it wasn't two steaks, a bottle of whiskey, and a blanket on the beach. But it was pretty darn close.

A lot has changed in world since the days of my friend's PT-19 adventures. There are fewer frontier spaces left to explore … especially a day's flight away from civilization. But fortunately, Baja is still Baja. It may not be quite as free and unpopulated as it used to be, but make no mistake about it, Baja California is still a frontier land. And while that poses a few more challenges in terms of weather, dealing with local officials, fuel, and maintenance, that's also what makes it an adventure. Besides. The challenges pale in comparison to the gifts that flying to Baja offers: unspoiled landscapes, baby whales, killer margaritas, white sand beaches, clear turquoise waters, sultry moonlit nights… and absolutely, positively, the best fish tacos this side of heaven.

Land of the Midnight Sun
CHAPTER THREE

The most significant and defining feature of Alaska is, quite simply, its size. It's a landscape on steroids; a wild land defying the sky to contain it, in a voice that resonates with a visceral, primal power. Nowhere else in America are humans so dwarfed by the land they make noises about inhabiting. I say "make noises about" because, even with all our modern technology and oil pipelines, humans have not yet conquered Alaska. They've made inroads, to be sure. But many of Alaska's cities ... including the state capital of Juneau ... are still not accessible by road. And from the air, the coastal settlements look like precarious toe-holds that the towering nearby mountains might shrug off their lower mantles at any time, flinging the human inhabitants back into the sea.

Nothing in Alaska is small. Not the mountains, not the

distances, not the hazards, not the moose, and not the mosquitoes. And living in the midst of such a massive, challenging wilderness, where darkness and light themselves don't even attempt balance, there's also a different standard for "normal."

On my first trip there, for example, I was introduced to the concept of "AFR" flight ... "Alaskan Flight Rules." Because the conditions and hazards are so much harsher than in the lower 48, Alaska Flight Rules basically consist of doing everything your primary flight instructor told you never, ever, ever to do. Things like scud running at 400 feet in low visibility above the ocean, navigating the fine line between hitting the towering mountains to your left and getting lost in low visibility over the ocean to your right by paralleling the ocean breakers just barely in sight off the left wing. Or flying in conditions that make Los Angles look like good VFR. (IFR routes in Alaska have to be high enough to clear terrain and get good radio reception, which often puts them in icing conditions above the mountains. So there's a lot of dicey low-level bush flying that goes on.)

During that first trip, at the very end of September, I saw the sun ... and the stunning mountain peaks surrounding us ... exactly one time in six days. But my second trip was the first weekend in May, to attend the Valdez, Alaska, Bush Pilot Fly-In. And that visit was a radically different experience.

For one thing, the sun was out in force. For three solid days. And at the beginning of May, each "day" lasts about 18 hours. The temperatures also hit an unprecedented 70 degrees, the skies were completely clear, and the winds were calm. For three solid days. You really have to have spent some time in Alaska, or talked to people who have, to understand what a miracle that represents. Especially on the first weekend in May. There were still huge piles of snow around, of course, which was a bit bizarre. But, again ... in Alaska, the concept of "normal" takes on whole new parameters.

Valdez, Alaska, is tucked up in the northeastern corner of Prince William Sound, at the southern terminus of the Alaskan pipeline. It sits on a placid blue bay surrounded by mountain peaks, and the area has a stark and powerful beauty to it that's evident as soon as you land and glance up at the 6,000-foot mountain ridge looming just north of the Valdez runway. But like the rest of Alaska, it's also a wild place, where 80 mph winds are not uncommon throughout the long, dark winter, the regional airline only makes it into the airport 65 percent of the time and, even by the beginning of May, all a pilot has to land on for 30 miles in any direction is snow.

Airports in those parts are scarce, and the terrain in between is pretty hostile. So even Cessna 172 pilots put skis or big tires on their planes, and pilots who routinely take on and master the land's formidable weather and terrain challenges can achieve the status of minor heroes. It would probably be a bit of a stretch to equate the Ellis brothers of Nesbena with Tiger Woods, Roger Federer or Eli or Peyton Manning, but famous bush pilots here do seem to command a kind of respect and reverence—at least locally—that approaches that of more typical sports heroes down south.

The bush flying competition at Valdez was interesting, in and of itself, with competitors arguing vociferously (as pilots are wont to do) about the best way to outfit and fly a plane for the best results. Some of the veterans told me they'd incorporated as many as 22 Short Take-Off and Landing (STOL) modifications on their small bush planes. When the competition dust settled, however, the short-landing champion wasn't one of the old hands, or even a pilot with a highly modified airplane. It was 22-year-old bush pilot from Wasilla named Matt Piatt, who managed to get his 100-hp Piper PA-11 down and stopped in a mere 99 feet.

Piatt's performance was impressive, to be sure— especially because it was on a hard surface, with no wind, on very warm day. But pilots at the fly-in were also quick to point out that none of the competitors' performances were really reflective of true bush conditions, where the planes are usually heavily loaded and those short field landings often take place at the end of tight, curving approaches through trees or other obstacles, and where the landing zones themselves are rarely straight and level. To really understand the challenges and the rewards involved, they said, you need to experience what all those modifications, skills and performance buy you, far from an airport ramp or competition chalk line.

So at 6 p.m., as the fly-in wound down to a close and the northern sun began to think languidly about moving slightly down and to the west in the still-bright springtime sky, I climbed into a big-tire Super Cub to go flying. This is not something you want to do with just anyone, mind you. Skills honed in the lower 48 are not adequate for the backcountry here. Local knowledge, a humble sense of respect for nature, and razor-sharp airplane skills are as essential for survival as fuel in the tanks. But the pilot I was flying with was a former professional bush pilot/guide named Mike Stitzel, who'd been flying in Alaska for many years and had won the short field landing competition at the fly-in the previous year. I was in good hands.

The first sign that I was with a bush master was when Mike called our departure from the taxiway, put the power up and simply took off *across* Valdez's 150-foot-wide runway, straight toward that aforementioned mountain ridge. We immediately turned west and hugged the ridgeline's slopes as we made our way toward the nearby Shoup and Columbia glaciers.

Bush pilot/guides like the Super Cub because they need an aircraft that maneuvers well at slow speeds and close to terrain in order to spot potential game targets. It's a kind of flying that takes some getting used to, however, as snow-covered ridgelines loomed beside us, in front of us, and then passed beneath us close enough to take my breath away at the sudden dropping-off of the earth as we sailed past their jagged, rocky peaks. As he flew, Mike pointed out several bears moving around on the really, really nearby slopes of the ridgeline north of Valdez. It was a little weird to be looking straight out of an airplane window at a bear, but there you have it. Welcome to Alaska.

Mike and I climbed toward the Anderson Pass, which separates the smaller Shoup Glacier from the expanse of the massive Columbia Glacier, which lies slightly further to the west. As we climbed, we entered a surreal world of drooping snow overhangs above deep, clumped-up, and untouched snow fields that looked very much like a real-life version of the Grinch's cartoon mountain hideaway. The only marks on the snow beneath us were from wind, snowfalls or avalanches, and any semblance of civilization seemed a distant, disconnected memory.

As we cleared the pass, however, all intelligent thought left my brain. Ahead of us stretched the 330-square-mile ice flow known as the Columbia Glacier. And the Columbia Glacier is a landscape for which there are simply no adequate words. As far as the eye could see were chunks of ice—some of them 2,000 feet thick—that had been forming and moving toward the ocean for more than 10,000 years ... ever since the days of the Ice Age. Fissures and crevasses of blue ice opened up everywhere beneath us, leaving pools of clear, turquoise water that Mike said was the most delicious taste on earth, if you could stand its almost-painful chill.

An engine failure here would be sporting, to say the least, although Mike pointed out several small patches of snow where he said he could put the Cub down safely. Looking down, I understood quite well why pilots around here take their short-field landing skills so seriously.

We flew along the glacier's face, which was an impossibly massive wall of ice that stretched miles ahead and behind us and towered several hundred feet in the air. Nothing makes you feel so small as flying right in front of a glacier's face, several hundred feet above the water, and still having to crane your neck upward to try to see the top of the icy cliff. Or makes you feel the sheer force of nature's power so viscerally as hearing a crack as loud as lightning and then watching a huge chunk of that ice, larger than most skyscrapers in Manhattan, break off, or "calve," from the wall and collapse with a deep, shattering BOOM! into the blue water below.

It's the scale that's so impossible to convey. When we attempted to take some air-to-air photos in front of the glacier the next day, it proved all but impossible to capture both the airplane and the wall in one image. If we shot the airplane in front of the wall large enough to see the plane, we got such a small piece of the wall in the photo that it didn't even begin to do justice to the grandeur and enormity of the setting. If the photographer captured the full width and height of the wall, the plane became an indistinguishably tiny little dot against it. Joe Prax, the talented local photographer who shot photos for me during the weekend, finally had to put the subject plane close to the photo plane and a long distance away from the glacier, in order to get both of them in the frame at the same time.

But on this flight, Mike and I didn't have to worry about photos. We were just out to explore and enjoy. After a couple of passes along the Columbia's face, we turned and headed south over the iceberg-strewn bay connecting the glacier with Prince William Sound. We passed pine trees and white, snow-capped peaks as we flew toward a tiny beach on a small spit of land known as Heather Island, a short distance in front of the glacier. As we circled toward the island, I looked down in awe at the icebergs and water beneath us. The water was such a clear shade of green that I could see the ghostly white mountain slopes that plunged deep beneath the "tip of the iceberg" pyramids rising above the water, conveying a startling sense of three-dimensional depth and strength.

Mike curved around a rocky point of land at the tip of the

island, dodged some pine trees, and straightened out just as he touched down on a short, sandy strip of the stone-covered beach. We were down and stopped with at least 100 feet to spare. Piece of cake. Mindful of our limited time and the requirements of my job, I jumped out of the plane and immediately started setting up for some photos.

I hadn't gotten very far when Mike came over and touched my sleeve. "Stop," he said. I gave him a blank and slightly confused look. "You'll get your photos," he answered gently. "But just stop for a bit, first. *Be* here. *Listen.*"

Mike grabbed our jackets from the plane. "Come on," he said, gesturing toward the beach. "Walk with me a bit." We hiked up the beach to the northern point of the island, where I entered a world more surreal, and more beautiful, than any I have ever known.

The clear blue and green water that stretched between us and the blinding white face of the glacier was filled with a thousand translucent ice sculptures, each carved into a unique and exquisite design by the forces of time, wind, and weather. A couple of sea otters swam leisurely around the nearer ones, and the retreating tide had even left a few sculptures perched jauntily on the edge of the beach. An artist couldn't consciously have created a scene this perfect if she had tried.

I sat down quietly on the stone pebbles of the beach and, as instructed, listened. The only sound that reached my ears in the stillness of the place was a remarkable and melodious symphony composed entirely of water. There was the steady gurgle of water flowing past the icebergs and the exclamation cracks of ice breaking away and falling with a splash into the waters below. There was the patter, gulp and splash of the otters' strokes, the dripping notes of ice drops melting in the sun, and the distant rush of glacial water cascading through the trees behind us. As wild as this place was, it had a peace about it that was contagious, extraordinary ... and so profound it resonated through me like a powerful, reverberating bass note. This kind of beauty wasn't something you *saw*. It was something you *felt,* throughout every cell of your body.

I turned and found Mike watching me. "It's a special place here," he acknowledged, with the understatement of someone who understands, and who sees that you understand, all that words could never convey about a place, experience, or moment. It was also a place, he might have added, accessible only to those who could land a Super Cub in less than 300 feet.

After lingering on Heather Island for a while, we traveled on and visited a number of other stunning places, flying high over mountain peaks and low over swamp grass, brown bears, and hatcheries of kitiwas and seagulls on stony beaches strewn with remnants of oyster and clam shells. We watched the sun get low in the western sky sitting on another grass-and-shell beach with the incongruous name of Hell's Hole—a name, I told Mike, that I suspected the locals chose to keep too many outsiders from coming in and spoiling its remote beauty.

I still have two perfect white, fluted shells from Hell's Hole beach sitting in a place of honor on my bedroom bureau, just so I don't ever forget that the rare and silent beauty of that evening. Because by the time we finally made our way back to Valdez, I was aware that I hadn't just had a great or memorable flight. I'd been given a gift few humans get to experience—

an intimate encounter with the song of life that runs through the earth with humbling power and soul-stirring beauty.

The weather in Alaska may be harsh, the mosquitoes huge, the winters long and dark, and normal landing sites few and far between. But what an acceptance of all those challenges—as well as big tires, a long prop, and a lot of practice in short field landings—buys you is something even more valuable than a set of Bushwheel tires. It's admission to some of the few remaining places on earth where nature, in all its wildness, power, beauty and mystery, still sings a song of miracles with a true and unspoiled voice.

It's a song whose magic could light even the darkest winter night... and a song that every Alaskan bush pilot gets to know by heart.

Cub Dreams

CHAPTER FOUR

There's a scene in the movie *Always* where the character played by Richard Dreyfuss, newly deceased, is asked by a friendly angel if he remembers learning how to fly. Wistfully, Dreyfuss looks down on a small Champ flying low over the midwest wheat fields, banking lazily in the summer sun. Yes, he says with a nostalgic sigh and smile, he remembers.

No matter how much more capable and efficient airplanes may have gotten in the years since World War II, there is still something irresistible about an old, classic Cub or Champ flying low over the landscape. It's an image as iconic as the sandlot baseball field or the corner ice cream parlor; a Norman Rockwell symbol of a simpler era, when planes were crafted from wood and fabric and pilots flew closer to both the earth and sky.

Once upon a time, of course, there was nothing nostalgic about Piper Cubs. They were the ubiquitous civilian pilot trainer; a common sight at airports all over America. Seventy years later, however, they're a lot harder to find. Every now and then, I'll sight one at a large, municipal airport. But for the most part, they've retreated into places outside the mainstream; little county airports where flying is still about more than utility. Airports like the one in Hamilton, Ohio, just north of Cincinnati.

Hamilton Airport was started as a family venture, back in the late 1920s, by the four brothers and one sister in the Hogan family. By the time I got to know it, Hamilton was a publicly-owned airport, but it was still run by the Hogan family, and it still had the feel of a family homestead. Bernie and Bill Hogan were even still working and flying there, along with several of their children.

Bernie Hogan ran the maintenance shop at Hamilton— still housed in the old, low-ceilinged cement and wood hangar the Hogans had built back before the war. The back storeroom where Bernie kept all his hardware was a throw-back maze of narrow aisleways between tall wooden sets of drawers, each drawer with a little brass pull handle and label announcing what obscure old airplane part or connection it contained. The room had a weathered, slightly musty smell that reminded me of my grandfather's garage, and walking into it was like walking into a living history museum.

Of course, the same thing could have been said of the whole airport. For tucked into the old corrugated tin hangar rows were more antique and classic aircraft per square foot than anywhere else I've seen outside of the show aircraft areas at Oshkosh. There were Stearmans, Champs, Globe Swifts, Cubs and various other fabric-covered Pipers from a PA-12 to a stubby little Colt, a Howard DGA, a Corben Baby Ace, a Bensen gyrocopter, a Taylorcraft, and even a side-by-side Aeronca Chief. One of the Hogan sons ran a cargo business out of the field with a fleet of Beech 18s and DC-3s that he parked on the grass at the end of the tie-down areas. The field even had a North American T-6 Texan and P-51 Mustang.

The Mustang was owned by a local foot doctor named Ron Runyan, but he let Bill Hogan fly it whenever he wanted. Bill, who'd owned a P-51H for years and did one of the most beautiful aerobatic air shows in a Mustang you'd ever want to see, would come out of the main office every now and then, hands in his pockets, and look up at the sky as if sniffing the wind and weather. Then, if we were lucky, he'd say, "You know, I think it's a Mustang kind of day." Almost before the words were out of his mouth, an ever-ready group of enthusiastic helpers would be heading over to Ron's hangar to get the Mustang out. Bill would fire up the old fighter in a smoky cloud of throaty engine noise, take off gracefully, gear coming up over the runway, and proceed to give all of us a breathtaking air show of high-speed low passes, loops and rolls, up close, personal, and just for the joy and the fun of it.

But what Hamilton Airport specialized in, more than any other old airplane model, was Waco biplanes. Cabin Wacos, Taperwing Wacos, UPF-7s ... every day at Hamilton was a Waco family reunion. Once a year, of course, there really *was* a Waco Reunion on the field—the official one, which brought

Wacos in from all over the country. That was really something to experience.

Hamilton, you see, was a small airport. It had a single, 5,000-foot runway, with an unofficial grass strip in between the runway and the taxiway. Just beyond the runway, looking across the strip from the bench outside the airport office, was a ridgeline that paralleled the runway, several hundred feet high. One end of the runway ended in a road that had been altered to wind its way around the airport when the strip was lengthened, some time back. Except for the runway, taxiway, a few short hangar rows and a very small ramp area in front of the office, the airport was covered in grass, including most of the transient parking spaces. Despite whatever changes had come over the years, Hamilton had retained the unmistakable feeling of a place tucked cozily into the land surrounding it.

So when dozens and dozens of Wacos descended on the place—accompanied, of course, by Waco-loving pilots in all kinds of other tailwheel (and even nosewheel) aircraft—it had a much bigger impact than it would have at one of the large, sprawling tarmac-covered airports in California.

Waco Reunions were always a good party, with pilots hopping rides for the fun of it all day long. I even got a ride from Bill Hogan in a visiting Waco, one time—a Taperwing model, as I recall. I also recall the snap rolls we did over the field. You don't forget your first encounter with snap rolls.

But of all the flights I ever took out of Hamilton Airport, the one I remember most occurred in the midst of a much more everyday aviation gathering: a weekend airport barbecue. Barbecues and gatherings at Hamilton weren't organized affairs, except for the Waco Reunion. Nobody said ahead of time, "Hey, let's do a barbecue every other Saturday!" It just happened, organically, because everyone was at the airport, anyway. And when I say everyone, I mean everyone. Not just the pilots, but spouses, siblings, families and friends.

I don't know how Hamilton evolved as the community park and playground for the families of the pilots who flew out of there, but I suspect it had to do with the Hogans, and the kind of people they attracted. Old airplane lovers, you see, are poets at heart. They have to be. Nobody else would choose to spend hours recovering and maintaining an old Cub or Chief instead of replacing it with a faster, lower-maintenance Cessna. And poets, when they gather, share the secret of a gentle heart, no matter how much they mask it in wisecracks and laughter. As a result, there's a warmth in their company; a shared friendship that needs no words, but draws even outsiders with its glow.

There was just so much warmth, laughter and goodwill at Hamilton, you wanted to be a part of it. Nowhere else was as fun on a Saturday or Sunday afternoon. And because of all the grass, shrubbery and history there, Hamilton was a more beautiful and homey place to spend some time than a lot of airports could claim.

On a typical summer weekend at Hamilton, a visitor would find more than just airplanes flying around. They'd find kids playing on the grass and riding their bikes around. They'd find non-flying spouses and friends sitting on lawn chairs, visiting and enjoying the lush beauty of a summer afternoon slipping languidly by. They might even find some of those spouses and friends joining in the more active fun—on and off the ground. Someone, for example, had drawn up a series of large poster-board score cards with various single-digit numbers on them. So every now and then, a group of friends and family bystanders would grab the cards and line up by the runway, offering every arriving pilot an Olympic-judge-style rating on their landing. The Hamilton folks were tough markers, as I recall. Zero was not an unheard-of rating. But the reactions they got, especially from pilots who'd never encountered a welcoming committee like that before, were priceless.

Because the pilots at Hamilton valued friendship and community, they also tended to outfit their hangars with hospitality supplies. Everyone, it seemed, had spare lawn chairs, refrigerators full of lemonade, barbecue fixings, watermelon and beer, and either a fire pit or barbecue grills outside the hangar doors. And as afternoon moved toward sunset, hot dogs, hamburgers, chicken, corn, potato salad and other munchies would begin to appear, almost as if by magic, on picnic tables around the hangar rows. Sometimes it was at Ron's hangar, sometimes it was at the fire pit down on Pete and Jeannie Reed's row. But food and people would just start to congregate, and soon it would be a party.

The flying that took place at Hamilton wasn't something separate from all of this; it fit in and around all the rest of the fun. Moved by the impulse, pilots would just pull out their airplanes and look around, see if anyone else wanted to go along, and take off into the afternoon sky for a while. And in the golden hour before sunset, the still evening air would always be broken at least once by the distinctive *chk ... chk ... chk ...*

kaCHIKA-chika-chika-chika-chika-chika sound of a Cub, Waco or Aeronca sputtering to life as someone took off to go touch and taste the sky for a few minutes before rejoining the party on the ground.

Which is how I got my very first ride in a Piper Cub.

The Hamilton family actually rented out a Piper Cub on the field, but I was still paying off my private pilot training, that first summer at Hamilton, so I didn't have any money to rent anything. One of the other Cubs on the field, however, was a clipped wing J 3 owned by a guy named Mark Taylor. He had it out on the line on Saturday afternoon, and I was walking around it, peeking inside and admiring its simple beauty.

"You like it?" Mark's voice startled me from behind.

"It's beautiful," I said. At Hamilton, you didn't have to say more.

We talked about Cubs for a little bit, and he showed me some of the things he'd changed or fixed on the plane. He said something about the way it flew, versus a regular Cub, and I confessed that I wouldn't know the difference, because I'd never been in a Cub.

"You haven't?!" he exclaimed, as if I'd just said I'd never seen fireworks, or eaten a two-scoop ice cream cone. "Well, then, we should go flying!"

He didn't need to press the suggestion. A few minutes later, I was folding myself into the front seat of the Cub and Mark was firing up the engine.

A Cub is a very simple airplane design. It has a very narrow, tube-and-fabric fuselage, and its two seats are "tandem," or one in front of the other. Most straight Cubs come with a 65-hp engine, although some have been retrofitted with 85 or 90 horse engines. But even with a small motor, the plane is so light that, for center of gravity purposes, a pilot flying alone has to fly the plane from the back seat. Cubs also don't have flaps and, unless it's been modified, a J-3 Cub doesn't have an electrical system. You hand-prop the propeller to start it.

But the most distinctive and, in my opinion, the best quality of a Piper Cub is its door. Unlike most airplane doors, which open like car doors, a Cub door is split horizontally. The lower half is covered in fabric, and the upper half is a Plexiglas window that can be lifted up and hooked onto a catch on the lower side of the Cub's wing, even in flight. But a Cub can be flown with the lower half of the door open, as well, leaving one side of the airplane wide open to the sky. And if you really want to feel the air you're flying through, the left side of the fuselage has a sliding window that can also be opened, leaving almost as much of the cockpit open as covered.

It was a warm, summer afternoon, and Mark left both the window and the door wide open as we lifted off Hamilton's grass runway. We banked sharply away from the ridge and headed out over the Ohio farmland. North of I-275, the circle freeway around Cincinnati, the nature of the land quickly changes from suburbia to farm country. Most of Ohio, in fact, is rural—giving the state some wonderful and beautiful areas to explore by air.

We stayed low, which is where a Cub was meant to fly. We banked gently over cornfields and hayfields, low enough that I could smell the green scent of the crops in the air coming through the cockpit. The clipped wings of the Cub gave it a much sharper turning ability, and we carved circles over barns and watering holes, meandering our way across the farmland like riders on a magic carpet, looking down on the lives of everyone beneath us.

It felt surreal to be so close to the earth and yet completely free to move at will above it. I could reach my hand out to the right and dip it in the currents of the sky as they streamed past us, sending eddies of swirling air through the cockpit itself. I could smell the earth below us, and watch the individual movements of the people on the ground. And yet, the laws of gravity that held all the other Earthlings to the planet did not, at the moment, apply to us. With a slight touch of the stick, we could bank straight across a cornfield, turn back over a copse of trees, dive down into a riverbed, or pull up higher over farm buildings and hilltops. Like Mary Poppins, we could drop down into the colorful landscape painting beneath us and watch it come to life, or pull further away and view it from afar.

After a while, Mark turned away from the open fields and dropped down into a winding river valley he said he knew well. Banking sharply left and right around the turns in the river was like riding a motorcycle with wings—a quiet, gentle motorcycle, with more grace than horsepower, but still nimble, quick and smooth as it leaned into each turn. And as we came around one corner, we saw a group of people fishing from the riverbank up ahead. They looked up and waved as we passed, and I put my hand out the window and waved back. They laughed and waved even more enthusiastically.

I was in an airplane, supposedly detached from the earth and everything on it. But far from disconnecting me, the Cub had brought me closer to people I otherwise would never even have seen, let alone had a reason to share such a lovely moment of greeting, laughter, and grace.

A little bit further downstream, we left the river and dropped down low over a field of grain that was moving in the afternoon breeze. The effect, as seen from a couple hundred feet in the air, was of waves rippling through the field. "Oh!" I thought as I caught my breath. "This is why they sing about amber waves of grain!" I'd known the lyric for years, but I'd never seen the effect with my own eyes, from the air, before. Beautiful was right.

I've had the good fortune to have had quite a few Cub flights since then. But none has topped that first one. Like Dorothy stepping into the Technicolor world of Oz, that first Cub flight opened up a magic carpet/sidewalk painting world that remains, to this day, my favorite place to visit. Especially in a Cub, because the airplane doesn't get in the way. With the door down and the window open, you can almost forget the airplane is there. And because a Cub flies so slowly, you have enough time to absorb the details of the earth below you, even when you're close enough to have far more detail to absorb. A Cub also has the advantage of being able to land almost anywhere, if you had to.

But that particular Cub flight was also special because of where it took place. Not Ohio in general, but Hamilton, in particular, where giving someone a ride in your Cub (Stearman, Waco, Aeronca, Piper) was just a normal part of a summer afternoon. Where flying was more about beauty and friendship than bragging rights or adrenaline. And where almost every pilot had a little bit of poet in them, somewhere. I've flown with test pilots, stunt pilots, jet jockeys and incredibly professional instructors. But a ride with a pilot who possesses a poet's heart is a uniquely memorable treat. They fly with care and love in every turn, and they show you the world through an artist's grateful eye.

When Mark and I landed, there were kids playing on the grass, and the barbecue fixings were making their way onto tables outside of hangars. Even as our engine stilled into silence, there was another *chk ... chk ... chk ... kaCHIKA-chika-chika-chika-chika-chika* sound of someone else starting up to go look at the sky before calling it a day. There was laughter, warmth, magic, and joy.

Most of us are granted only a handful of moments in life where we wouldn't have changed a single molecule, even if we could. And even those slip away all too quickly, like all the other moments we're given. All we can do is try to be so present in those perfect moments that the knowledge and memory of them registers firmly and clearly in the film of our mind's eye, so we can carry them with us as we travel forward in time.

Fortunately, I paid attention on all those summer weekends at Hamilton. And my memories of the days I spent there, and that very first Cub flight, make up a cherished mosaic of a special time and place I was just lucky enough to stumble onto, once upon a time. The airport has since changed, and the people have moved on. But those memories will remain with me, like the scent of the summer crops wafting through the Cub's cockpit, for the rest of my days; a reminder of how much magic and perfection can be found in unexpected places, everyday moments, and the world as seen through a poet's eyes.

A World Apart
CHAPTER FIVE

The first thing most visitors learn about Sudan is that nothing in its landscape is steady or easy ... either geographically or politically. It's the largest country in Africa, encompassing almost a million square miles, much of which is difficult to traverse. There are few roads, especially in the less-developed south, and the majority of the roads that exist are not paved. Large sections of Sudan have an arid desert climate—hot, dry and dusty for most of the year. Along the Nile River and in sections of the south, the land is greener. But during the rainy season, much of the country becomes impassable for weeks or even months on end, with little clumps of raised grass dotting an otherwise muddy and watery landscape.

Sudan is also home to the Sudd—one of the most notorious and noxious swamps in the world. Famed pilot and writer Beryl Markham, who was the first pilot to fly the Atlantic east to west, and who wrote *West with the Night,* described the Sudd as "twelve thousand square miles of swamp that seethes and crawls like a prehistoric crucible of half-formed life." It is an example, she said, "of the less attractive by-products of the Nile River, and one place in this world worthy of the word 'sinister.' Add to that, 'eerie' and 'treacherous,' and any other similar adjectives that occur, and the conception may become clearer."

Sudan's challenging geographical landscape is one reason aviation plays such a big role in getting goods and people around the country. The other is Sudan's even more challenging political landscape. Conflict between the Arab north and the African, tribal south dates back to the time of the ancient Egyptians, and tension between the country's Islamic and Christian movements dates back to the 7th century. Of course, the "country" as it now appears on a map is a product of European/Egyptian treaties signed in the late 19th and early 20th centuries and modified by a British-imposed plan for Sudan's independence after WWII. The British plan initially called for Sudan to be split into two separate entities, but the plan was changed at the last minute to stipulate that the north and south would be unified and governed from the north.

And therein lies the main root of the trouble.

The first round of Sudan's civil war started almost as soon as independence was declared, and the conflict has continued almost unabated. In the years between 1955 and 2005, there have been just 10 years of peace. And that's not even counting the side conflict in the Darfur region. Civil war between the south and north flared up again in 1982 and continued until the peace treaty of 2005, during which time several droughts exacerbated the humanitarian crisis that almost always accompanies the ravages of war.

The non-stop conflict and intense, layered humanitarian and natural disasters in Sudan led to the start of an international airlift effort that has been ongoing now for more than two decades. It's expensive to transport goods and people by airplane, especially in regions where everything from fuel to replacement parts has to be shipped in from long distances. You do it only when ground transportation is impractical, either because the geography is too challenging, or the political conflict in the area makes it too dangerous. In Sudan, both reasons apply.

The first time I flew into Sudan, it was an unexpected side trip to an article I was writing on bush flying and poacher patrol in the game parks of Kenya. I'd met a couple of pilots in a coffee house in Nairobi who said they were flying relief missions into Sudan and invited me to come flying with them. Always up for a new exploration or adventure, I said, "Sure!"

The phrase "ignorance is bliss" comes to mind, when I think back on that moment. I had no idea what I was getting myself into. And even if someone had told me, I'm not sure I could have imagined it well enough to understand. In any event, a few days later I found myself in a borrowed pilot's uniform, standing on a dusty ramp in the desert outpost town of Lokichoggio, Kenya, just south of the Sudanese border, wondering what other or parallel universe I'd just wandered into.

The airport itself reminded me of something out of the

television show *M*A*S*H,* with its canvas supply tents, rickety control tower and sense of urgent mission. But the general atmosphere and surrounding buildings, where transient pilots and misfits marked time and sought relief from the oppressive desert heat with Tusker beer beneath slow-turning ceiling fans, were straight out the movie *Casablanca.*

But surreal as the surroundings may have been, the mess of the situation itself was far worse. The main relief effort was run by the U.N. World Food Program (WFP). But the U.N. could only fly into places where the Government of Sudan gave them permission. The Government of Sudan, of course, was also one combatant in the civil war; actively opposed to having any aid reach its southern adversaries. So the U.N. program was restricted to mostly northern-held towns. As a result, a "renegade" relief effort had sprung up in parallel, with mercenaries, non-governmental organizations and missionary pilots flying unauthorized missions into villages and towns held by the southern Sudanese forces.

One consequence of that set-up was a bizarre juxtaposition of opposites, where mercenaries and missionaries lived and flew side by side, and where pilots would gather together under one of two thatched-roof bars to drink together at night, only to get up at dawn and fly support for two different sides of a war. And while the mercenaries quipped that if this war dried up, "there's always Congo," there was a discouraged sense of fatigue in many of the pilots' eyes. When I arrived in Lokichoggio, the war had been going on for 18 years, with more than 2 million people already killed and still no end in sight. The south was adamant about not submitting its largely

African/Christian (or animist) population to the north's Arab/Islamic rule. But the south is where the oil is. And the north had no intention of giving the oil fields up.

I came back from that trip with a newfound understanding of how intractable and complex the world's problems are, and a discouraged heart in terms of any hope for Sudan. But four years later, in large part because of international pressure, a peace accord was finally signed between the north and south, with an intermediate power-sharing plan and elections scheduled six years later to allow the country to decide for itself whether to stay unified or separate into two different countries.

Key to that agreement, however ... and to successful unification of the country behind a governing plan ... was the south's charismatic leader John Garang. The Arabs respected him and the southern tribes had learned to obey him. Tragically, he was killed in a helicopter crash a mere five months after the peace accord was signed. Clearly, the accident reduced the chances of success significantly, but many in the war-weary country still hoped the peace would hold; that some agreement or electoral solution could prevail.

It was against all of this history, and all these hopeful and heartbreaking turns of events, that I decided to return to Sudan in 2007. First and foremost, I wanted to see what difference peace had made to ordinary people in the country. Six years earlier, the people in the southern villages we visited had been cowering from northern attacks in Antonov AN-32 bombers ... airplanes that flew overhead and rolled home-made bombs (55-gallon drums filled with explosives and improvised shrapnel) out the back cargo ramp and onto targets that included schools, because if you kill and maim the children, you destroy the parents' willingness to fight.

Do you recover from that kind of trauma? Is peace even possible after a generation of war? Is hope? I had no illusions of getting a definitive answer; at best, I hoped to gain a few isolated glimpses into the lives and hearts of people who had suffered more than my imagination could begin to embrace. And the best way to accomplish that goal was with an airplane.

To visit a variety of people from different tribes and areas of Sudan would be Herculean task on the ground; impossible at certain times of the year, and both grueling and time-consuming even in the dry season. So to help my chances of getting back to Sudan, I got checked out in the Cessna 208 Caravan—a beautiful and practical airplane that combines the reliability of turbine power with really good rough and short field performance … and which I knew was used by a number of relief organizations flying in Africa.

The Caravan was popular in places like Sudan, because most of the runways there are three shades below "unimproved." It's not just that many of them are short and poorly maintained, although they are. Or that many bear a closer resemblance to a challenging dog-leg, Par 5 hole on a golf course than anything one would term a runway. Or that they're often cluttered with people, animals and other obstacles, and sprinkled with deceptive areas of "black cotton" soil, which turns into a morass of spongy goo when wet. Or that fuel is a scarce, "bring your own" commodity, in a country filled with some seriously hostile terrain. It's the *combination* of all of those things that makes flying in Sudan so hazardous. And that's not even counting a complete lack of weather forecasting and other information available to pilots there, or the oppressive heat, dust and primitive conditions on the ground. Or, as I was soon to discover, persistent security concerns in some places, despite the official peace.

The hazards of Sudan are not a challenge an inexperienced pilot takes on by themselves and lives to tell about. But with my Caravan proficiency in hand, I arranged to do some co-piloting with a non-profit organization called Air Serv International, which provides aviation services to secular humanitarian organizations all around the world, and which operated several Caravans in Africa. As it turned out, however, while I flew with Air Serv in Chad, Uganda, and the Democratic Republic of the Congo on that trip, my flights into Sudan were with different organizations.

My first two legs into Sudan were with a commercial cargo company called 748 Air Services, named after the Hawkers the company initially flew in Kenya and Sudan. Rumor has it that 748 was the inspiration for the cargo company in Phillip Caputo's novel *Acts of Faith*, which was set in the complex aid and gun running world of Sudan during the war. But by August 20007, 748 was primarily engaged in supplying commercial and NGO-subsidized goods to rebuild villages and towns destroyed in the conflict.

In an ironic twist, 748 had also acquired several of the AN-32 bombers used by the north to terrorize the south during the war, and the company was now using them to bring in life-saving, instead of life-threatening, cargo. The world tilts on a dime, and one side of the mirror is not always that far from the other.

So my first leg into Sudan was actually in an AN-32 cargo/bomber. We took off at dawn and flew several hours to reach the village of Nyamlel—a closely grouped gathering of thatched-roof huts just south of the Darfur region. Nyamlel, like many villages, had been completely leveled during the war, and all its residents had scattered to refugee camps or, in the case of the men, into the Sudanese People's Liberation Army (SPLA). Several young men I talked to there were in their 20s and could remember nothing except a time of war. Most of them had been fighting since they were 13 or 14.

A group of pre-teen and teenage boys, entranced with my digital camera, approached and showed each other, pointing and laughing, their images frozen instantly on its back screen. In that moment, they were normal kids; curious about something new in the world, teasing and laughing with each other over their shows of bravado or shyness.

Clearly some of them had had some education somewhere along the line, because several of them spoke a little English. And our cargo in the AN-32 was a load of furniture for a school the village was rebuilding. So I asked the boys what they wanted now that there was peace in the country. I imagined I might hear about dreams of learning, or even farming and families. But as soon as I asked the question, the laughter stopped. Their faces got deadly serious. One of the boys, who looked about 14, reached out, took the pen out of my hand, wrote the word "INDEPENDENT" very clearly across his palm, and held it out to me.

"But what if the vote isn't for independence?" I asked.

"Then I'll take my gun and go to my place," replied one of the boys, who looked to be in his late teens. I asked where "his place" was, but he shook his head with a frown. There were things outsiders were not to know.

In the village of Boma, I asked a woman, through a translator, if she thought the peace would hold. She pressed her hands together as if praying. "It has to," she said, with eyes that spoke of more painful memories than I had the heart to ask her to recount. But in that same village, I asked the same question of two older men, who were showing me the wreckage of a small Piper shot down by northern soldiers, and asked if they thought the northern Government of Sudan would hold to its side of the bargain. They shrugged. "If they don't, we'll make them," they said, with a simplicity of tone that was disturbing. The prospect of war had become so commonplace that it was simply a fact, not even warranting a rise in voice or emotion.

In all the villages I flew into, the responses followed in a similar vein. People were returning, schools and huts were being rebuilt, and life was struggling its way back to normal. Children could now walk to school without fear of being bombed, one woman explained. Small stores and other kinds of commerce were beginning to crop up around the country. In Juba, the provisional capital of South Sudan, a huge open-air market was thriving on a piece of land that, as recently as two years earlier, had been a minefield. But at the same time, the peace was clearly fragile. The men and boys didn't seem to be bothered by the idea of taking up arms again; indeed, they seemed more comfortable with their roles as soldiers than with any peacetime vocation.

There were also issues of reconciliation in places where the population had been split in its partisan support. After a couple of days with 748, I connected with the pilots I'd flown with six years earlier. They flew for AIM Air, a missionary flight service organization based in Nairobi, and they flew a variety of aircraft, including Cessna Caravans.

Denny Dyvig, an impressively talented pilot as well as a thoroughly good-hearted human being, came up to Lokichoggio specifically so we could fly together again. We spent two days touring numerous villages in southern and central Sudan, overnighting in the town of Kauda, tucked up in the Nuba Mountains north of the Sudd.

Kauda was the equivalent of a Mason-Dixon state in the U.S. Civil War, with Arabs, Africans, Muslims and Christians in a mixed population that divided painfully into opposing sides during the war. It was also just a few miles from the mountain hideout of the SPLA's commanders, so it was bombed mercilessly throughout the conflict. As a result, the entire town, which was large enough to support churches, mosques, and brick structures, had fled. Its former inhabitants were now returning, and there was a souk (market) again in the town's central plaza. But as a woman told me that night, there were scars from the past that the town had still not figured out how to heal.

"People forgive, but they do not forget," she said. "There were people who turned in their neighbors, whom people still call 'murderers' under their breaths. It is very difficult to come together as a community again, after what's happened."

Especially, she might have added, because it turns out

that violence as a solution to disagreements, once learned, is a very difficult habit to break.

Our last stop before returning to Kauda that night had been a tiny village called Jalud—a challenging destination in war *or* peacetime. It has an elevation of 2,000 feet, a rough and almost-indiscernible dirt runway that changes heading more than 10 degrees in its 750-meter length, a tall ridgeline close in to downwind and a mountain less than a half mile off the end the strip. And on that particular day, it also had 95-degree temperatures and thunderstorm cells bearing down on the field. Consequently, our unloading process there was charged with extra haste and tension, because every second brought the cells closer. If we didn't get out in the next few minutes, we probably weren't going to—at least, not before the thunderstorms hit. In the civilized world of paved runways and malaria-free accommodations, we might even have entertained the more relaxed notion of waiting the rain out. But in Jalud, it would have been days before the airstrip dried out again. And Jalud, Sudan isn't exactly a place one wants to be stuck.

"Okay, once we start, we're not stopping," Denny cautioned as he hustled into his seat, latched his door, and cleared me to start the engine. We ran through an abbreviated checklist and I bumped the throttle forward as Denny called out taxi directions. "Avoid those clumps of grass, those are soft spots," he warned as we began to move across the soft vertisol. "Green clumps means there's water there ... and watch that, there, that's a thorn bush, don't hit that, it could give us a flat tire." I swerved left and right as best I could while keeping the yoke full aft and trying to guess where the sidelines of the runway lay.

We reached what seemed to be the end of the runway and I swung around toward the darkening eastern skies, pushing the throttle forward as I turned. We broke ground, banked sharply right away from the black clouds and lightning flashes, and started getting the gear, flaps, and trim all set for climb and cruise. But just as I was beginning to breathe a little easier, the HF radio crackled to life. The connection was scratchy— not surprising, given that the dispatcher was located in Nairobi, more than 1,100 miles away. But we could hear urgency in his voice.

After several frustrating back-and-forth transmissions to confirm our location, we heard the dispatcher say, " ... we have a ... *crackle* ... situation ... *crackle, crackle* ... hos ... *crackle* ... need you ... *crackle, crackle* ...*" The voice broke up in the background static.

Denny looked at me, frowning. "Did he say 'hostage?'" he asked. I shook my head, unsure.

"I thought he said 'hospital,'" I answered, "but it could have been 'hostage.' Or 'hostile.' What do we do?"

"I'll call him on my satellite phone when we land at Kauda," Denny replied. "We'll go from there."

"What if the place he's calling us about IS Kauda?" I asked.

"Don't think so," Denny said. "We were just there an hour ago."

"And they shot eight people near there two months ago."

Denny nodded "I'll call ahead before we land, but I think we're okay."

Half an hour later we landed without incident in Kauda, and Denny called base on his satellite phone while I worked with the ground crew to refuel the Caravan. He walked over as I climbed down from the fueling ladder.

"Well, turns out it was hospital *and* hostage," he said. "They've had a kind of mutiny or uprising at a hospital in the village of Akot, south of here. The SPLA apparently has it subdued, but they want us to go in tomorrow morning to pick up the hostages."

The next morning, Denny and I were up well before dawn. We got an update confirming our mission and that the army did, in fact, have the situation under control. Then, as the sun broke over the mountain ridge east of Kauda, I lifted the Caravan's nose off the grass and dirt surface of the runway and turned south. En route, we flew over the reflective water and dense forest of the Sudd. Looking down on its thick, tangled and clearly inhospitable terrain, I decided Markham knew what she was talking about.

As we closed in on Akot, we were getting security updates every 10 minutes. We stayed high as long as possible, just in case there was any ground fire, and then dropped steeply toward the end of the runway. I taxied quickly to the end of the strip, where our human cargo had been told to await us. The previous year, Denny had been doing a medevac from a nearby hospital strip when the patient and staff were ambushed by an opposing tribal group as they were headed out to the plane. The ambushers shot the patient dead as a nurse tried to carry him from the car. Even though we'd been assured that order had been restored here, Denny didn't want us near the hospital, and

I heartily agreed with him.

We were carrying a passenger from Kauda and, as we landed, he said he had to get out and pee. "You have 60 seconds, and we'll leave without you if you're not back," Denny cautioned sternly as he unbuckled and went to open the back door. Less than five minutes later, I had the throttle at full takeoff power and we were climbing steeply away from the airstrip.

It was only as we reached a safe altitude and I began to breathe normally that it hit me. I'd been to Akot before. Six years earlier, Denny and I had flown a Cessna 210 into this very same strip. And we'd had to do a quick turn then, too—because we were flying into a war. A wave of sadness came over me as I realized the irony of our rescue. South Sudan was no longer at war. But an absence of war does not necessarily equate to peace.

For some, a trip containing such aching moments of heartbreaking realization and such difficult and uncomfortable challenges would not be a cherished memory. But despite all the uncertainty and trauma there, I actually came away from Sudan with a renewed sense of hope about the human race. For the struggles of the Sudanese to rebuild after so many years of war, especially in the face of continuing tribal conflict, uncertainty, and the looming prospect of renewed warfare, showed a strength and resiliency far deeper than I had imagined possible.

Indeed, the most encouraging stop of my trip was at a Darfur refugee camp, among people whose entire villages had been burned to the ground as residents were raped, killed or hunted down into the bush. When the refugees arrived in the camp in 2003 and 2004, I was told, they were among the most ravaged of any refugees the aid workers had ever seen. They died faster than medical workers could clear away the corpses.

And yet, three years later, despite continuing uncertainty and deprivation, new life was finding its way into the survivors' hearts. There were brand-new babies and families, and mothers and children were laughing and playing together. The scars are eternal and run deep, I'm sure. The women said they still dreamed of their old villages, even when they were awake. And they still mourned the lost. But here, they said, they felt safe. And with that precious measure of safety, they were able to regroup, love, and move forward again. Leaving the camp, all I could think was, if these women can continue on, seeking life and love again after all they've lost and endured, what *can't* the rest of us get through?

Flying into Sudan was not easy. In order to connect with the people there, I had to consciously resist the impulse to turn away from the darker scenes and sites of human conflict, struggle, and pain. I had to will myself to walk forward, eyes open, and allow the darkness to surround me and assault all my senses. But it was worth it. Because once my eyes adjusted to the dark, I also began to see things I might have missed in the glaring light of day. Including just how powerful and enduring the human spirit can be.

For all its discomfort, flying in Sudan was an incredibly rewarding experience that left me with far better understanding and respect for the maddening and marvelous complexity of the world. We may be a species capable of horrifying violence and harm. But we are also a hardy lot, with layers of strength, beauty, and resiliency I never could have imagined in the safety of my living room.

And somehow, that gives me hope.

Lone Star Surprise
CHAPTER SIX

"I have one bad word for you," my friend told me.

I'd just announced that I was planning on flying my Cheetah, solo, from southern California to Key West, Florida. I hadn't flown solo across the country before, and I was a little apprehensive about the challenges I'd encounter, despite my excitement about the guaranteed adventure the trip would provide. A VFR, transcontinental flight in a slightly under-powered, under-instrumented piston airplane with no autopilot and an average speed of 105 knots is nothing if not an adventure. If I flew two three-and-a-half hour legs a day (beyond seven hours, I'd discovered, hand-flying gets tiring enough that mistakes start to creep in around the edges), and the weather cooperated, the trip would take me a mere ... *six days.* Across two mountain ranges, desert, swamp, dense forest and barely cultivatable southwest flatland.

The possibilities for trouble were endless. I wracked my brain trying to imagine what hazard my friend had in mind. Thunderstorms? Boredom? Mechanical trouble? Airspace or controller nightmares? I gave him a concerned and questioning look.

"Texas," he said with a grin. "You'll be three days getting across there."

It wasn't the first time I'd heard disparaging words about the Lone Star State. The cracks pilots have about flying across Texas are so numerous and oft-repeated they could easily pass for urban legends. To pilots who get their satisfaction from waypoints passed and borders crossed, Texas presents a torturous, marathon nightmare. Not only is it inexplicably huge, it also encompasses hundreds and hundreds of miles of unbroken and uninspiring flatlands where the only notable landmark features are a few circular irrigation fields and as many oil wells per square mile as there are apartment buildings in Manhattan.

Truth to tell, I also had my own memories of droning interminably across West Texas in my old Cessna 120 (which makes the Cheetah look positively zippy), struggling to stay awake over the endless brown landscape, and wondering: a) why ANYONE would live in this place and b) if we would ever hit the New Mexico border. So it was with more than just a little trepidation that I passed through the last of the New Mexico mountains and crossed into the great, wide, state-with-no-end.

West Texas is one of the very few places I've flown in the

United States where fuel stops are actually a serious issue. In Mexico, your fuel gauge is your primary instrument, because airports are widely spaced and fuel is not always available at every airport. But in the United States, there are generally any number of options along any route. The question isn't which one has fuel; it's which one suits your schedule and routing best.

West Texas in a slow piston airplane, on the other hand, presents something of a challenge. I either had to stop far sooner, or a bit longer, than I wanted. The Cheetah has 52-gallon tanks, so I generally give out before the fuel does. But the longest leg I've ever flown in my Cheetah was in West Texas, just trying to make the fuel stops work.

But just because there's not a lot of populated terrain in the southwest corner of the Lone Star State doesn't mean the landscape is unremarkable. One of the first surprises I found, upon crossing into El Paso's airspace, was that the local scenery was far more varied than the flat, barren wasteland I remembered. Granted, the land surrounding the Salt Flats VOR, east of El Paso, is pretty bleak territory, worthy of the name. But just to the north, jutting majestically out of the desert landscape, are the towering rock formations of Guadalupe Peak. (Salt Flats was apparently built in the early 1930s as an emergency landing field, with a radio range navigation aid that predated the VOR, after an American Airlines flight crashed in the Guadalupe Mountains.) I had difficulty tearing my eyes away from the stark, imposing beauty of the mountains' rusty red cliffs and peaks, and I found myself looking back even as they receded into the distance behind me.

East of Guadalupe, the summer thermals rising off the dry land began to intensify. Cumulus popcorn clouds dotted the sky above me, dribbling my plane like a basketball as I made my way slowly across the arid landscape. Turbulence has many manifestations, and the "basketball dribble" variety isn't one of the scary types, but it still gets old after an hour or two. So by the time I spotted the town and airport of Pecos, Texas, on the horizon, I was more than ready to set the Cheetah down for a while.

To say that Pecos is a quiet little airport is like saying that the Himalayas are pretty tall hills. My flight guide reported Pecos as having fuel, but I began to question my choice as circled over what appeared to be a completely deserted airport. Finally, I spotted a fuel truck parked in one corner of the airfield. If the airport had a fuel truck, I figured, it probably had someone who knew how to use it. I cut the throttle and banked into the traffic pattern, calling out my position despite a ghost-town silence on the Unicom frequency.

I landed and taxied toward what appeared to be an FBO in one corner of the field. As I approached, a woman came out of the building and gestured me toward a tie-down spot. She had the wings tied down before I even had the mixture pulled back, and she greeted me with a friendly smile and a surprisingly crisp British accent.

"We sometimes get dust devils through here, so I like to get the wings tied down quickly," she said by way of explanation. "Welcome to Pecos. I've got to go fly, but my husband will take care of anything you need. Just make yourself at home." Another quick smile, and she was off toward the few weathered-metal T-hangars sitting a little ways down the ramp.

I had just been greeted by Isabelle Blanchard … the owner, chief pilot, flight instructor and one half of the line crew at the Pecos Air Center.

I was raised in the New York metropolitan area, and I still have a deep appreciation for the diversity, color, energy and sophistication of the world's great cities. But my flying life has taken me to far more rural and out-of-the-way places and has helped me appreciate the very different kind of treasures that bloom there. I still have a cherished photo of myself in Deming, New Mexico, taken on a long cross-country flight in my old Cessna 120. I'm leaning jauntily against the 120's cowling in front of the Deming terminal, which consisted of a small stucco building with a hand-painted sign above the door that read: "Welcome to Deming, NM. Home of pure water and fast ducks." How can you not love a place that advertises the speed of its ducks? (Deming's other airport landmark was its courtesy car: a 1962 Econoline ambulance that was missing part of its floor, not to mention second gear.)

Pecos, Texas didn't have any ducks. But it did have killer homemade burritos in the fridge that sure beat the peanut-butter cracker sandwiches at many other FBOs around the country. I went inside and met the other half of the line crew: Isabelle's husband Dennis. He told me the story of how he'd taken six flying lessons from Isabelle, married his flight instructor, and "has been pumping gas ever since." Besides pointing out the burritos, he offered me the use of a majestic old Dodge Diplomat boat that was masquerading as a car, out behind he office. He sent me off with advice on where to eat, what to see in town, and told me to "make myself at home" when I returned.

My plan was to let the afternoon thermals settle down a bit before heading out again. So I had a few hot, summer hours to kill. I asked Dennis if it was safe to leave the Cheetah's canopy open a little bit, to keep the inside from baking in the mid-day sun. He looked insulted.

"Yes, ma'am," he drawled. "We don't have people bother things here."

I asked him where the keys to the car were kept. He looked at me with a look that was half incredulous, half confused.

"They're in it," he answered, as if there were no other option. I smiled. We each have our own frame of reference on the world; what's expected, what's normal, what's safe. You can even begin to believe that your own particular frame is the only one, if you don't get out of your element every now and then to see what other people's norms are. An airplane doesn't *force* you to look at the world through different lenses, of course, but it can take you to places where they're a lot easier to try on. And sometimes, like a visitor in a *Twilight Zone* episode, I feel as if my airplane has planted me in a completely different culture ... or time ... from the place I departed only a few hours before.

As I maneuvered the Diplomat toward the main street in town, I noted that the trust Dennis placed in his fellow citizens might also have something to do with the fact that justice here might still be meted out with the ruthless authority of the old-time Wild West. Painted above the wide doors of a building by a large, central, outdoor arena were the words "Reeves County

Sheriff's Posse." I wasn't sure what that consisted of, exactly, but I could well believe that they'd still hunt you down with horses and six-shooters around here.

Pecos, Texas was, after all, the inspiration for the "Pecos Bill" character of cowboy folklore fame. According to a sign at the entrance to the town, it's also the "Home of the World's First Rodeo." I'm not sure about the "world" part of that ... the gauchos of South America might argue that point. But Pecos was apparently the first U.S. town to hold a "public cowboy competition where prizes were offered."

I wandered through the local museum, ate lunch, and drove around all the streets I could find. But it doesn't take all that long to see all that Pecos has to offer, and it was still hot and sleepy as I made my way back to the airport. Dennis and Isabelle were gone, but they'd left me a note reiterating their request to make myself at home, with their home phone number in case I needed anything. I'd been there less than three hours, and I already felt attached to the place. It wasn't fancy, but it was personal. Warm, welcoming, authentic and personal. If only there were more places like that in the world.

I bought a Coke, which at the Pecos Air Center still cost a grand total of 50 cents. That alone was a museum moment, harking back to the once-relevant but now long-outdated saying I learned as a kid: "That and 50 cents will buy you ...". In most places, even in the year 2000, I'm not sure what 50 cents could have purchased. Here, it got you a long, cool, draught of refreshment, which I enjoyed while stretching out on a sofa underneath a ceiling fan. I dozed off there while the afternoon heat beat down on the landscape, finally rousing myself about

5 pm for the next leg of my journey.

The heat had dissipated a bit and the air was far smoother as I headed south toward San Antonio, even though dappled shadows from small popcorn clouds still dotted the landscape. Just like the land around the Guadalupe Mountains, the landscape here was a far cry from barren. For mile after mile, I flew over stunningly artistic folds of mesas and hills whose shadows and contours stood out even more dramatically in the late afternoon light. Texas, like the larger country it's a part of, is clearly more multi-dimensional than outsiders might imagine. But the beauty of this part of the Texas landscape would be invisible from an airliner, and hard to see clearly, or at least as completely, from the ground. My airplane might have been second-hand, but the vantage point it granted me was one even first-class passengers rarely got to see. It's a vantage point reserved only for birds and a few lucky people known as pilots. And it was a gift well worth enduring a little heat and basketball-dribble turbulence to obtain.

I landed in San Antonio just before dark and found more Texas hospitality awaiting me. The Raytheon FBO I chose was awash with fancy jets, but the line service person who guided me to a parking spot, and who introduced himself as Jerry, had a twinkle in his eye as I cautioned him about towing the Cheetah with its castering nose wheel.

"Don't you worry. I know how to take care of Grummans," he said with a wink. "We have three based here."

Wow. A jet FBO with people who still liked lowly little Cheetahs. I left my plane in Jerry's capable hands and walked inside, where a logistics goddess named Dawn got me a killer deal at a super hotel right by the Riverwalk in downtown San Antonio. An hour later, I was sitting at a candlelit table in an outdoor Riverwalk café, eating crab cakes and salad with a glass of great wine as the warm evening air moved gently through my hair. Warm, desert nights aren't as sultry as in the tropics, but they have an exotic feel and beauty all their own. They also have a lot fewer mosquitoes.

After dinner, I wandered up from the RiverWalk to the Alamo. It was almost 11:00 at night, but I'd never been to San Antonio before, and I was leaving first thing in the morning. So I figured I'd at least take a quick look at the historic landmark from the outside. The building was smaller than I expected, and I commented as much to the night guard by the wall. He explained that the "Alamo" building was actually only one part of the original fortress, and he suggested that I come back in the daytime, when I could get more information. I thanked him but explained I was only in town for the night. He nodded with regretful understanding. Then, looking around at the deserted area in front of the landmark, he said, "Well, I could give you at least a bit of a tour, if you'd like?"

Which is how I got my own personal tour of the Alamo and the spots in the compound where the epic battle took place. And in the silence of the night, with the dramatic spotlights shining up on the adobe walls, I was able to step out of the modern world far more easily that I ever could have during the crowded daylight hours. As my guide talked me through the evolution of the battle, I imagined the sounds, the sights, the chaos, the fear, the slash of the swords, and the smell of the musket smoke. I might not have gotten the whole daylight tour … but I *saw* the Alamo.

As I walked back to my hotel room, looking forward to the huge and heavenly bed that awaited me there, I realized that I had been in San Antonio less than four hours. And I was already having one of the most magical nights I could remember.

But it was the next morning that Texas truly took hold of my heart. San Antonio had some clouds lingering around 2,000 feet, so I leveled off at 1,500 feet as I headed out of town. The controllers steered me around all the military airspace east of San Antonio and then explained that their radar was down in the next segment, so they wouldn't be able to see me or provide any services until I was 40 miles west of Galveston, on the eastern Texas coast. They wished me a good flight and signed off.

For a moment I just flew along as the controllers' words sunk in. They couldn't see me. Not even if I wanted them to. I looked around, and a grin spread slowly across my face. The clouds had dissipated, the sun was shining, the early morning air was smooth perfection, and I had just been handed a get-out-of-school-free card. I looked down at the green fields beneath me and suddenly felt … *way* too high. I dropped down to 1,000 feet and looked again. Still too high. I checked the chart. No towers to be had, no towns in the vicinity, and landing fields as far as the eye could see.

Life was good.

My grin got wider as I dropped down another few hundred feet and started to play. I circled left and right. Did some S-turns over a tree line. Turned and followed the curves of a small river as it wound its way south. I wasn't technically *headed* south, of course, but that seemed like an unimportant detail at that moment. I practiced turns about a cow, waggled my wings at a farmer plowing his fields, and did figure eights over a limestone quarry swimming hole. Before long I was laughing and singing aloud in the cockpit, bubbling with fun and joy as I wandered and played above the landscape.

"Ah, yes," I remembered. "THIS is why I learned to fly!"

I caught sight of another airplane in the sky ahead of me. "Wow!" I thought. "Another pilot, doing the same thing that I am!" I smiled and climbed a bit, banking away to give him some more space. As I passed, I took a closer look and realized my play companion was actually a crop duster. In that moment, I fully understood the appeal of his job, although I felt sorry that he (or she) had to pay attention to annoying details like straight lines.

I flew on, banking away from a flock of thermalling birds and circling around the town of Wharton, Texas. The town behind me, I felt way too high again. I dropped down lower, finding more rivers, ponds, and fields to explore, all the while remembering just how much I loved flying like this. I'd almost forgotten. It's also the kind of flying the Cheetah does best. She may not be the best platform in turbulence, but my, oh my, she maneuvers well! And she was as happy as I was that morning. I could feel it in her wings.

At the rate I was going, it was going to take me forever to get to Galveston, of course, but I didn't care. I was having fun. More fun, in fact, than I could remember having in a very long time. My heart was light, my soul was singing, and I felt as if I could fly on like this forever.

I silently thanked my airplane, the world and yes, even the

state of Texas, for granting me this gift of sunshine, laughter, and pure, unadulterated joy. And for reminding me ... through the feel of the Cheetah's wings banking around bends in a river, the sight of a bright yellow crop duster, and the perfection of green fields lit up by a golden morning sun ... that enjoying the journey is a whole lot more important than any goal or destination.

By the time I reached Galveston, I'd shed a tired skin I didn't even know I was wearing, and I couldn't wipe the grin off my face. I fueled, got something to eat, and headed north toward New Orleans. The undeveloped Gulf coastline in Texas is beautiful, and I flew along it between 500 and 1,000 feet on my afternoon leg. But even that beauty couldn't match the perfection of the morning.

Twenty-six hours after entering the Lone Star state, I crossed into Louisiana. Twenty-six hours overflowing with hospitality, friendship, beauty, magic, history, laughter and joy. As the Texas beaches receded behind me, the words of my friend echoed again in my head. "You'll be three days getting across there ..."

A mere three days? Shucks. I could have gone on like that forever.

Thirty Miles an Hour over Italy
CHAPTER SEVEN

Sometimes, all it takes to sell an idea is a single sentence.

"We'd like to know if you'd have any interest in writing an article about flying one of our blimps."

Flying a blimp, to my way of thinking, falls into the same kind of once-in-a-lifetime, irresistible, attention-getting idea categories as landing on a glacier, touring the South Pacific in a flying boat, or flying a U-2 to the edges of the atmosphere. Maybe someone would answer "no" to a question like that. But not anyone I know. Especially after hearing the sentences that followed:

"We've got a couple of cross country trips I think might work for you," the blimp company's president continued. "One is taking a ship from North Carolina to Ohio. But our sister company in Switzerland is also going to be taking a ship from

Switzerland to Athens, through the Alps, to provide security for the Athens Olympics. You could go along on that trip, if you preferred."

No disrespect to the great state of Ohio, but it wasn't like I really had to agonize over the choice.

Which is how I found myself standing on a street corner in Paris on the 4th of June, 2004, at the beginning of a trip that was supposed to last 10 to14 days. Kind of like how the *S.S. Minnow* was supposed to have a three-hour tour. But I get ahead of myself, here.

The Swiss blimp company, Skycruise Switzerland, actually had a contract to fly two airships to Athens for the Olympics: one to act as a sky camera, and one to provide an aerial platform for security cameras, sensors, and communication relays. What it turned out *not* to have, as of the beginning of June, was the promised *payments* for the flights from the Greek organizers. But I only found that out later. At the time, when I called the company's chief pilot and announced I was in Paris, getting ready to board a train for Switzerland, all I got was news that the departure had been a tad delayed, and a suggestion that perhaps I'd like to take a few days' vacation in Paris while they straightened out the departure paperwork.

Unfortunately, a few days' vacation in Paris wasn't in my budget—or *Flying* magazine's, for that matter. Fortunately, it just so happened that I had a friend from high school who was living with his family in Paris that year. So I called Lewis and Lili and asked if I could come sleep on their living room floor for a few days, and they said "sure." God bless good friends.

But as a few days stretched into a few more days, I began to get concerned about whether the trip was even going to take place. I didn't want to have to explain a wasted ticket to Paris to the home office. I called the chief pilot every other day, trying to read between the lines of his vague answers as to what the heck was going on.

Finally, just about the time I decided I was going to go to Switzerland anyway, plant myself in front of this guy and demand some straight, no-nonsense answers, he called to say the paperwork looked like it was straightened out. I took the next train out, overnighted in Geneva, and arrived the next afternoon in Lucerne, Switzerland, at the northern edge of the Alps' Gotthard Pass.

Where it then proceeded to rain for the next five days.

The rain gave me lots of time to read the local tourist pamphlets, which is how I discovered that Lucerne, Switzerland is known as "The Rain Capital" of Switzerland. Terrific. Considering that the blimp crew needed clear skies to get through the mountains, I realized that this trip might stretch out a lot longer than I'd planned for or budgeted. So I moved into the same set of low-rent accommodations as the blimp crew to save money while we waited. And waited.

Finally, the sun came out and, with great relief, we all headed out to the airport for a last test flight before launching for Athens. All went well as the ship's pilots maneuvered off the mast for their final control, balance and engine checks before takeoff. They ran up the rpm on the ship's two outboard "vectors"—two ducted propellers, powered by Porsche 230-hp engines that rotate up to 85 degrees up and 110 degrees down to help pilots hover, descend, and climb—for a final engine check. And then, suddenly, all hell broke loose.

With a horrible *BANG!* followed by a rapid, "BRACCCKKK - BRACCCKKKK - BRACCCKKK- BRACCKK-BRACCCKKK" clatter, parts came flying off the right-hand engine. The crew chief signaled a frantic cut-off signal, the pilots cut the power and, when the dust settled, we all moved closer to examine the damage.

It was bad. There were holes ripped through the cowling of vector mount, top and bottom, and the tubing inside was twisted like a pretzel. The mount was broken in three different places. The only piece of good news was that the blimp's helium bag hadn't been torn open by the flying shrapnel. A closer examination revealed that the solid drive shaft connecting the vector to the engine had sheared clean through—a failure nobody could recall any Skyship ever experiencing before, in all the years they'd been in service.

It was going to be a big repair—complicated by the fact that there was no blimp hangar in Lucerne, so all the work was going to have to be done with the ship on its outdoor mast. Which meant working on a target that swung as often and as in as many directions as the wind blew. The job was going to be further complicated by the fact that there were only five Skyship 600s in the world. So getting spare parts, especially on short notice, was going to be more than a little challenging.

The chief pilot shook his head in disgust. "It could be weeks," he said gruffly, as he headed off to start making phone calls. My stomach sank. I began to see my career, or at least my credibility as a tenacious, reliable writer who always brought the story home no matter what, dissipating in front of my eyes.

By that evening, however, we had a "Plan B." A group of us would go to Berlin, where the company's second airship was parked in a hangar. We could take that one to Athens while the first ship was repaired. Which is how I found myself, early the next day, in the right seat of a pick-up truck crossing north into Germany instead of in a blimp headed south for Greece.

Around dusk, we pulled into the small town of Krausnik, a handful of miles east of Berlin. The town, which was celebrating its millennial that year (a mind-boggling idea, in and of itself), still bore scars of damage from World War II and neglect from all the years since. There was also a memorial in the center of town, in Russian, with a translation to German, commemorating all the heroes of the Motherland who had given their lives in the great fight against Fascism, 1941-1944. Local residents were still tending to the memorial and planting flowers around it, 15 years after reunification. If you're ever tempted to think the world and the people who populate it are simple, spend a little time in places like Krausnik.

Later that night, I got a cheery email from *Flying*'s managing editor, asking if I was in Athens yet. After all, I'd been in Europe for almost three weeks. "No," I emailed back. "I'm in East Berlin." A pause. Then I added, "And if East Berlin doesn't seem like a logical stop in between Switzerland and Athens, it's because you don't understand airships as well as I'm beginning to understand them."

The good news was that all of that enforced down-time, in close quarters, gave me the chance to really get to know the blimp's pilots and ground crew. The ground crew consisted of mostly young men, from a variety of countries around the world from Bosnia to the Dominican Republic, who were looking for a steady job and a bit of adventure. The captains were older and had some really interesting and complicated back stories of their own. But the end result was a diversity of culture, language and worldviews that provided endless material for exploration and conversation. We even came up with our own version of "20 Questions," where we tried, as a group, to come up with 20 really worthwhile questions to ask each person, with the goal of discovering the most important parts of their life, experience, and beliefs.

The dynamics of a blimp crew are unusual in the "lone eagle" field of aviation. Unlike most other pilots, a blimp pilot cannot land without a crew—a *large* crew—to corral the airship and guide it safely onto a mooring mast. You may be the pilot in command, but you're still at the mercy of the winds, as well as the skill, dedication and quick reflexes of your ground crew, to take off or land safely. And with the rigors of being on the road together, the group can feel more like a big, boisterous family than just a group of paid pilots, mechanics and ground handlers.

After a day of flight tests, we took off from Berlin and headed back to Switzerland. Finally, more than three weeks after I'd landed in Paris, I was airborne in an airship. Even if we never left Lucerne, I could now make something out of the story.

But when we landed back in Lucerne. we discovered that the cavalry had arrived. The Pilatus Aircraft company has its headquarters in Lucerne, and the company had agreed to send a crew of wizard machinists, welders, and engineers across the field to work with the blimp crew to build a new mount and shaft for the blimp vector and repair the other associated damage. They'd been at it night and day since we'd left, and the ship was now only a couple of days from completion.

The chief pilot decided to delay our departure so we could take the repaired, unmarked airship first, leaving the second ship, which had large company logos on its sides, to give tourist rides for a couple more weeks before following as the camera ship. So I was stuck in Lucerne with the crew for another 3–4 days. Desperate for a story, I took advantage of the crew's new Pilatus connections to help arrange a demo flight in a Pilatus PC-12 turboprop business/bush plane. The PC-12 is a beautiful aircraft, and I wrote a piece about the flight and sent it back to New York as a kind of good faith down-payment on the blimp story ... which I casually, and with fingers crossed, assured my boss would be following soon.

For once, the gods were kind. At 6:05 a.m. on the 4th of July ... a full month after I'd arrived in Europe ... we pushed back from the mooring mast and, blessed with clear skies and calm winds, climbed toward the Gotthard Pass, Italy, and the Athens Olympics.

Until that day, nobody had ever flown a blimp through the Alps. The reasons are varied. But the biggest one is a matter of physics. A blimp is a non-rigid envelope filled with helium. There are two flexible "ballonets" inside the envelope that can be filled with air, or emptied, to provide ballast in flight, and to keep the nose and tail of the ship balanced in climbs and descents. The ship also carries water ballast, but that's a one-time shot, as opposed to the ballonets, which can be constantly adjusted up or down.

The difficulty with crossing a mountain range like the Alps is that all gases expand with altitude. So in climbing to clear the mountains, the blimp would soon run out of air ballast. Once the air was pushed out of the ballonets by the expanding helium, the pressure in the helium would start increasing. To keep from exploding the bag, helium would have to be vented. But then, on the far side of the pass, the blimp would have to descend. Descending would cause the helium to contract again, leaving a far lower volume of helium in the bag. And since blimps depend on helium for both lift and structural integrity, that's a problem.

So it was a tricky equation, requiring us to take off with minimum cargo weight (I discovered that I equate to six bags of shot ballast), and minimum fuel, so we'd be as light as possible on the back side of the pass. There were also winds to contend with, and we had to send a portable mast and crew ahead to be waiting for us on the other end ... a day ahead of our departure, because trucks in Europe weren't allowed to travel on the roads on Sundays.

The Gotthard is the lowest passage through the Alps to the south, but we still had to clear 7,300 feet to get over it, even winding our way *through* the mountains instead of over them. The pass is also less than a mile wide in parts (hence the need for a no-wind day). But for all that had gone wrong, and *could* have gone amiss on that leg, the actual flight through the mountains went like clockwork. And sailing through the Alps at 30 mph, a few hundred yards away from snow-covered peaks, is a unique experience, not soon or easily forgotten. I'd flown through that same pass a few days earlier in the PC-12, but even at 100 mph, with flaps and gear out, it wasn't the same. It all went by too fast. The bad news about blimps is that you don't get anywhere very quickly. The good news is, you get to see everything along the way really, really well.

Four hours later, we landed safely at Locarno, Switzerland, a small town right on the Italian border. With the Alps behind us, we figured the rest of the journey would be relatively simple. But as it turned out, the challenges were just beginning.

Locarno, in fact, was a good indication of what was to come. Because we got there on a Sunday, we couldn't get replacement helium for the airship until Monday. We drove back to Lucerne for the night, but returned to the Locarno airport by 8 a.m. Monday morning, expecting a relatively prompt departure, only to discover that the helium company wasn't there yet. When the helium guy *did* show up, it took him more than three hours to refill the blimp. We loaded up and prepared to leave, but then one of our radio wires short-circuited, jamming all the transmissions in the area. By the time we got that fixed, it was 1:30 in the afternoon, and thunderstorms were moving in from the east. And since a blimp can't outrun much in the way of weather, we had to cancel for the day.

The three blimp captains and I then went in search of rooms for the crew—a daunting challenge in a small town when your crew consists of 20 people. We stopped at several modest establishment that didn't have any rooms. This wasn't looking good. The rain had already begun to fall when we pulled into the parking lot of a dingy, three-story, cinder-block structure that someone had told us might have rooms. I stayed in the Land Rover while the three pilots went inside to investigate.

When they came out a number of minutes later, they didn't climb in the car immediately. One of them leaned his head in my window.

"Well," he said, "they have rooms." I frowned. That should have been the end of the story. But he had a funny look on his face, and the other two pilots, standing a few feet behind him, were starting to snicker.

"So what's the problem?" I asked.

"Well," he chuckled, "*we're* okay. But we're not sure they're going to let you stay here."

The New Yorker hairs on the back of my neck shot up at the thought of being denied access to something everyone else was allowed. "What do you mean, they won't let me stay here? What the hell's wrong with this place?" I shot back indignantly.

"Well, that's the thing. The only problem with this place is ..." the pilot hesitated. The snickers behind him got more pronounced. "... it's a whorehouse." All three pilots burst into loud bouts of laughter.

Oh, dear god, I thought. How old *are* they? I'd spent enough time around them by then to know that they liked to give anyone they could a hard time. "You're just trying to get my goat," I said as I got out of the car and shook my head. I'd put a quick end to this. I strode purposefully into the lobby of the motel ... and stopped, dumbstruck.

The main lobby opened into a large bar, where a disco ball turned slowly above the red and purple trimmings, even though it was only two o'clock in the afternoon. Women in lots of make-up, very high heels, and very short skirts were negotiating with dowdy men in khaki or jeans pants. Money was changing hands. And then the men were following docilely behind the stiletto-stacked women right in front of me, headed off down the halls.

"We told you," one of the pilots said in my ear. "It's a whorehouse." No kidding. The rate, the working madam told us, was 80 francs for the room, 43 francs for the ... uh, room service. But it was the only place in town with 20 rooms for the night.

And so it went. En route to our next stop, in Brescia, Italy, our ground crew got lost, and then one of the trucks got a flat tire, so we had to circle for two hours while they sorted all that out. Another downside to blimp travel is that, no matter what happens, you don't get to land until your crew gets there. Period.

And yet, I didn't half mind the delay, because if the turbulence isn't bad, a blimp is a pretty wonderful place to spend some summer hours. The pilots, the chief engineer and I were the only ones on board, even though the gondola could seat at least 10 people (and had an on-board lavatory with its own window, which we took to calling the "loo with a view").

Our typical cruising altitude was between 500 and 1,000 feet, and we opened up all the picture windows along the sides of the cabin. So in between stints where I got to fly, I spent hours with my chin resting on my hand, my elbow on the window sill, gazing out at our shadow passing slowly across the vineyards, hills, towns, castles, cathedrals, and fields below.

As we waited for our crew in Brescia, we circled over Lago di Garda, northeast of town, and looked down at the legendary opera star Maria Callas' old home and the castle of a Renaissance lord who'd built his own private harbor, inside his castle walls, to house his personal Navy. History in high school was never as vivid, or as interesting, as this.

When you're actually flying a Skyship, you don't have quite so much time for sightseeing, because flying a seven-ton blimp can actually be a lot of work. A Skyship 600 consists of 245,000 cubic meters of helium and air, encased in a polyester bag 200 feet long, 67 feet high, and 63 feet wide. None of which maneuvers precisely or sharply. So flying an airship consists of coaxing it around the sky by moving four barn-door-size control surfaces at the tail. And since those surfaces are linked directly by cable to the yokes in the cockpit, without any boost or trim, moving them requires the energetic use of every single muscle in a pilot's arms and upper torso. Especially in wind or turbulence.

There are actually times, in smooth and calm air, when an airship requires almost no control inputs at all. But flying a blimp in any kind of thermal or wind activity is like trying to command a large, obstinate and powerful animal. Sometimes it feels like a trail horse that keeps straying off course, requiring repeated tugs on the reins to pull it back onto the trail. Other times, it feels more like a not-quite-broken horse that needs constant, energetic and assertive inputs to keep it under control. And in some truly frightening moments, it can turn on you like an angry, wild creature that is flat-out determined to trample

Lane standing on a stray iceberg on Heather Island, Alaska. ▶

◀ The face of the Columbia Glacier looms above Lane and Alaskan bush pilot Chuck McMahon as they fly past it in his Super Cub.

Photo credit: Joe Prax

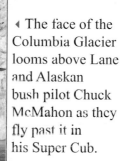

Lane and her Cessna 120 in Deming, NM— home of "pure water and fast ducks." ▶

◄ The gang at the Hamilton, Ohio airport scoring the landings of arriving pilots.

The California sunset reflected in the Cheetah's cowling after an evening coastal flight. ▶

▲ The entire village of Pieri, Sudan turned out to meet Lane on a refueling stop.

▲ Lane shares a light moment with some of the women she met in a Darfur refugee camp.

The one-word response by a 14-year-old to Lane's question of what he wanted, now that Sudan wasn't at war. ▶

▲ Lane and AIM Air pilot Denny Dyvig on her first trip to Sudan, in 2001.

▲ Lane in her Cheetah after making her way across the great wide state of Texas.

◀ Lane flying AIM Air's Caravan in the skies over Sudan.

▲ Lane with the "gold medal" blimp crew she traveled with from Switzerland to Greece.

▲ Lane flying the Skycruise Switzerland blimp over southern Italy, en route to the 2004 Olympics.

◀ The view out the side windows of the blimp going through the Gotthard Pass in the Swiss Alps.

▲ The blimp on its mast, getting refueled with helium, in Locarno, Switzerland.

◄ Lane celebrates her Jimmy Buffett flight down the Florida Keys at Capt. Tony's in Key West.

▲ Lane and her parents after she took them flying for the first time—15 years after getting her pilot's license.

◂ Lane (right, age 3) and her sister Gail modeling their new astronaut outfits on Christmas morning.

Photo credit: Dean Tokuno

▲ Lane in her real-life space suit.

◂ The view from the U-2 at 70,000 feet.

Lane taking notes in the U-2 cockpit, using a pencil from a special holder on the side of the yoke, and a board covered in green paper to avoid glare. ▸

Photo credit: Dean Tokuno

▲ Maj. John "Cabi" Cabigas congratulates Lane at the end of their U-2 high flight, surrounded by other U-2 squadron pilots.

you under its feet or buck you off its back entirely.

Blimp pilots have to develop a good sense of anticipation, because if you feel the ship starting to move, you have a window of about 1.2 seconds to get on the controls with gusto—to counter the shift. If you miss that window and the ship's 15,000 pounds of mass gets away from you, it can be the start of a wild ride, requiring a series of full-deflection control inputs—which means turning the yoke at least 20–30 degrees past a normal aircraft's aileron stop in both directions— to finally get it back where it started.

The force that requires, and the resistance of the ship's mass to control inputs, are both so high that a blimp is also literally impossible to over-control. Watching the pilots shove the yoke all the way forward and hold it there with a knee ramming it into the instrument panel was a little disconcerting ... until I found myself doing the same thing to generate enough downforce to get the ship to break out of a strong thermal.

And if all that activity is attention-getting in the air, it's ten times more adrenaline-producing close to the ground. Depending on conditions, landing and taking off in a blimp can itself be something of an Olympic sport. An Olympic *team* sport.

We finally landed Brescia and cleared customs and immigration, but we were then delayed for a couple of hours because we couldn't get take off clearance. Lord knows why. Perhaps the Pope needed to intervene. But that delay made us late for our next stop at the coastal resort town of Fano. We were pushing dark when we finally saw Fano on the horizon, which was a problem because night VFR flying in controlled airspace isn't allowed in Europe.

We called the airport "in sight" more than 15 miles away so we could close our flight plan in legal daylight, but it was full dark by the time we landed—which caused another set of problems, because blimps don't land on runways. They land into a "V" formation created by the ground crew, with the crew chief at the formation's apex. The crew arranges the V into the wind, and the pilots use the formation as a giant flight director, guiding their final descent, as the crew narrows the V more and more until, on the crew chief's signal, the crew breaks into a dead run to capture the guide ropes and the gondola side bars, wrestling the blimp to the ground and under control.

It can be a challenging maneuver even in daylight, because if the blimp is light, or the winds are up, the pilots have to descend under power and carry extra speed in order to get the blimp down. That, in turn, can lead to something the pilots refer to as "bowling for crew members," as the ground crew gets dragged through brush, dirt, and sometimes even up into the air as they struggle to get the airship under control. It's actually a very hazardous phase of flight, and some crew members have been seriously injured by a bucking blimp in windy conditions. A couple have even been killed, both because 15,000 pounds of mass packs a hell of a punch when it's got a good wind behind it, and also because a blimp can go from ground level to 200 feet up in the air in a matter of seconds.

A blimp might look like a cartoon aircraft, but it has the ability to morph almost instantaneously into a lethal wild animal, especially near the ground or on the mast. As a result, blimps actually have an emergency *takeoff* procedure that bypasses all the niceties and gets it off the ground, NOW.

At night, all those normal challenges just get magnified. We couldn't even see the V until the crew chief finally located some flashlights to hand out to the point people in the formation. We finally got down, got the ship moored, and went into town for a few hours' rest. The next morning we got to the airport early again … and had maintenance problems. By the time we got those straightened out, we couldn't get clearance to take off because we couldn't get clearance to land at Foggia, our next stop. Apparently, it was lunch hour there, and the airport was closed. And in Italy, lunch time lasts three hours. So by the time we finally got clearance to land, which meant we could take off, our little Garmin Pilot III GPS put our arrival at 6:50 p.m. Or, a mere 25 minutes before the airport in Foggia closed for the night. And since we didn't have clearance to land anywhere else, that was just too close to risk in a blimp. We turned around and headed back to Fano.

Despite all the frustrations of the trip, the crew managed to make the most of whatever hours we had in the towns we stayed in along the way. We'd scout out the "old town" sections of each city as we approached—easy to spot because the streets would wind tightly in narrow, crooked paths around a central cathedral and square, sometimes surrounded by old city walls. We'd note the location and head in that direction as soon as possible after getting the airship put away for the night. Sometimes, especially in Italy, where dinner typically extended over five courses and two hours, that meant we didn't get a lot of sleep. But it was worth it. In Fano, we sipped Caipirinhas by the beach and then went into old town, where we ate in an outdoor café and danced in a nearby square as local musicians played into the night. I doubt I could keep up that pace for any great length of time in my life, but on the trip to Greece, I functioned surprisingly well on only 3–5 hours of sleep a night. Like I said, it was worth it.

The next morning, we left for Foggia, blissfully unaware of the nightmare we were about to encounter. Because all of our previous adventures—including the whorehouse—paled in comparison to the seeming eternity we spent in the hot, lawless hell of Foggia.

The first sign of trouble was that, despite having advance clearances to get our crew on the field, the crew was first denied access, and then held at gunpoint in a hangar for over two hours while we circled overhead in 106-degree temperatures, roiling thermals, and 25 mph winds. Which, in a blimp highly susceptible to winds and thermals, was something way short of fun.

When we finally got permission to land, the high winds made it one of our most difficult touchdowns, dragging the crew through a very rough and bramble-filled field before we finally came to a stop. Then, as soon as we had the blimp on the mast, soldiers with guns approached, took our passports and threatened to arrest the five of us in the blimp, declaring that we were in the country illegally. We had stamps in our passports from Brescia, but that didn't seem to matter.

We were all perplexed. Foggia was supposedly a civilian airport. But we'd landed in the middle of a deserted, overgrown facility that was crawling with camouflage-clad soldiers with automatic weapons, flak jackets, and no sense of humor. Something wasn't right about the place. It had the feel of a Stephen King novel, which wasn't exactly reassuring. And the only person we had on the crew who spoke fluent Italian was a pilot from the Netherlands. A brief, animated discussion ensued between the Dutch pilot and the chief engineer, who was from the Dominican Republic, before the pilot went off to try to negotiate our release.

"They want money," the engineer argued. "We just need to pay them off."

"No, no," the pilot insisted. "They say it's a paper-work problem."

"That means they want money!" the engineer retorted in frustration.

The Dutch pilot disappeared with one set of officials and guards, while another set remained to guard the rest of us on the blimp. And then, while we waited on board to see if we were going to be arrested, we got hit with the dust devil.

Any high wind condition is extremely hazardous in a blimp—especially when it's moored on the mast. Seven tons of fast-moving mass is nothing to take lightly. And a twisting wind can get a blimp moving from zero to 35 mph across the ground in less than three seconds, then spike the ship straight up on its nose before throwing it out the other side of the thermal. At that point, the blimp can crash back down to the ground—potentially hard enough to break the propellers and other components, not to mention inflict serious injury on any poor soul still on board.

So there we were. One second, I was sitting on a relatively

sleepy airship, swinging languidly in the hot afternoon breeze. The next, I was in the belly of an angry whale that was rumbling like a freight train as it picked up speed across the ground, getting ready to breach, and the chief engineer was yelling at us to get off the ship … *NOW!*

Unfortunately, the wind was pushing the blimp in the same direction that we had to exit. So we had to hit the ground running, as it were, to clear the blimp's path, and it was about four feet to the ground, which was moving disconcertingly fast by the time I jumped.

I didn't make it.

My right foot hit an uneven patch of thorny ground, and I fell hard, with seven tons of aircraft coming close on my heels. With no other choice, I rolled flat and covered my head with my arms as I felt the gondola whisk by close above my head. From a distance, I heard the crew's cries of "One Down! One Down!" as the guys came running.

Fortunately, one of the people on board was the chief pilot, who got to the cockpit, got the control lock off, and managed to fly the ship out of the thermal, keeping it from going up on its nose or crashing back to earth. It was all over in less than 15 seconds. But by the time I shakily got to my feet again, I had a whole new level of respect for these deceptively innocuous-looking aircraft.

In the end, we weren't arrested, although we were taken to the police station offices and detained until 8:30 that night. In addition, our generator was stolen, and our passports were only returned after almost three more hours of negotiations the next morning. So it was with no love lost … and still no answers as to the mysterious happenings that transpired there ... that we left Foggia behind us the next day and headed south to Taranto, at the southern tip of Italy.

Taranto was our last stop before heading east across the Adriatic Sea to Athens. So we had to wait there for a day while part of our crew took a mast and headed to Greece ahead of us, because we had to have a mast waiting for us there before we could leave the one we were moored to in Italy.

There was one other panic moment when, as we crossed the Italian coastline, we were informed that our clearance into Greece had expired due to our many delays, and that if we attempted to enter Greek airspace, or land at our destination without not only an ATC clearance, but a *diplomatic* clearance, we would be arrested.

"Oh, dear god, who *isn't* trying to arrest us?" I asked the chief pilot in exasperation. "Tell them to take a number." He laughed.

"So what the hell is a *diplomatic* clearance?" I asked.

"I don't know," he answered, "but we have to go find one."

"What are we going to do in the meantime?" I pressed.

The pilot grinned. "Keep going," he said. "At 30 miles an hour, you have some time to sort things like this out."

Ah, the beauty of blimps. Nine hours and one fully certified diplomatic clearance later, we crossed the Corinth Canal and entered the Athens Bay, only to hit the worst turbulence of the entire trip. The only warning was a slight shudder in the ship as we brushed against the tentacles of wind at the edge of the whirlpool. Then, almost before we could react, the churning waves of air coming off the mountains of

Athens grabbed hold of us, and the airship pitched sharply upward and yawed to the right before turning and diving in the opposite direction toward the sea beneath us. Everything not tied down went flying. The maneuver felt very much like a wingover—except, of course, for the fact that we didn't have wings. The chief engineer and I battened down the hatches and strapped ourselves in as tight as we could, as the two burly captains alternated flying in 10-minute stints, because fighting that kind of turbulence was too exhausting to manage for any longer than that.

I began to feel an odd sense of kinship with Ulysses himself, battling the gods through seemingly never-ending challenges before they allowed him the prize of a safe landing on Greek soil. In the end, we endured the pitching and rolling waves of air for three full hours before the crew, rushing to Athens from our intermediary emergency landing site, arrived at the field just as darkness fell, and we struggled back to earth again—grubby, exhausted, but still proud of our accomplishment.

We arrived in Athens *six weeks* after I arrived in Paris, and the journey itself had taken us nine days and 44 flight hours, not counting the side-trip to Berlin. The car trip back to Switzerland took only 35 hours, total. But I wouldn't have traded that flight for the world.

For one thing, there is nothing—and I mean nothing— quite like seeing the world from an airship. We cruised through the Swiss Alps, the hills and medieval fortresses of northern Italy, the Adriatic coast, and the blue-green coastal waters of Corfu and Greece a mere 500 to 1,000 feet above the ground, drifting slow enough to wonder why that guy didn't put skylights on his converted WWII pillbox-house, and low enough to read a cathedral banner proclaiming its 500th anniversary. There were more than a few moments of excitement, of course. But there were also moments of exquisite serenity, my head and arms resting on the edge of the Skyship's huge, open picture windows, a gentle summer breeze pulling at my hair, as I watched the sun sink into the Adriatic Sea.

And while we endured more than a little discomfort along the way, it was discomfort shared—among 20 remarkable human beings, all working together to get everyone safely home each night and one step further in our journey, no matter what challenges, sweat, cursing, laughter, frustration or exhaustion that entailed. Imagine, for a moment, how it feels to have a friend waiting for you at the end of a tough flight. Now multiply that by 14, and you'll have an idea how it felt to see the crew lining up to bring us home at the end of every day: sprinting to catch the ropes, throwing themselves through the gondola doorway for extra ballast, running to aid a crew member in trouble, and allowing themselves to be dragged through brambles and thorns rather than to let the ship get away or into danger. A few mountains, miles, winds, whorehouses, dust devils and even armed commandos all become manageable if you have that kind of company to face them with.

I went to Europe thinking that I was going to have the fun of flying a blimp for a while. I left knowing that I'd had the privilege of being part of a blimp *crew* for a while. A crew that, if they ever make airship cross-country an Olympic sport, would be a formidable favorite for the gold.

The Calm after the Storm
CHAPTER EIGHT

I've often said that if it weren't for the darkness of night, we'd neither have, nor appreciate, the splendor of sunrise. And I unreservedly believe that sentiment to be true. But I also recognize that even if it's true, it's still sometimes cold comfort when dawn is hours away and the cold, loneliness, and fear that come with the darker moments in our lives make us wonder if we'll even make it to sunrise in one piece. On the other hand, if we do make it, the light that follows seems more pure, more lovely, and more precious by far because of what we had to fight through to get there. We may not be able to avoid the storms. But we at least seem to gain a greater capacity for joy in the wake of our tougher struggles. Which is something, even if we can't fully appreciate the gift of it in the middle of the fight.

Over the years, the Cheetah and I have gone more than a few rounds with darkness and danger, especially when weather moves in. On more than one occasion, I've even had the distinct feeling that either she or I have some kind of supernatural ability to change the weather. Generally for the worse. I'm not kidding. I've ended drought in three states, just by flying there. For four days on one long cross country, no matter where I took the Cheetah, I ended up in the middle of a big, red, moving dot on The Weather Channel maps that noted the location of the very worst weather in America. It's more than a little annoying, seeing as I am, by choice, a strictly VFR (good-weather-only) pilot. But if I could hone this apparent talent into something predictable, I could probably make good side money as a rainmaker.

In any event, it was with this knowledge that I asked a line guy in St. Augustine, Florida one time to put my airplane in a hangar, right after arriving for an overnight stop. I was on my way to Key West, Florida, and I'd just spent the day dodging build-ups and low visibility all the way from Pensacola.

"But we're in the middle of a drought!" he protested. "It hasn't rained here in months!"

"Yes, well, that's about to change. *I'm* in town," I said with a wry smile.

"Seriously. Flight service says there's zero chance of precipitation tonight or tomorrow," he replied.

"Buddy, all I know is what I saw coming in here. And a few lessons from hard experience. Humor me. Put the airplane in a hangar."

He shrugged and acquiesced. I went off to the friend's house where I was staying that night ... and woke up in the morning to cracks of lightning, thunder and sheets of rain pounding down on the roof.

Two days later, the weather cleared enough that it appeared a departure might be possible. I called Flight Service the night before, and they advised an early departure. In Florida, at least in June, thunderstorms tend to build up over the ocean during the night, and over the land during the day. But in this case, a tropical depression had left a truly ugly weather pattern sitting over the northern part of the state (hence the rain), with bad weather everywhere. If I left early and went inland a bit, however, it appeared I could make it through the weather before the build-ups got too bad. Then, once I got to southern Florida, the skies looked a lot clearer.

I got up at dawn and called Flight Service again. The same advice prevailed. I got out to the airport and called again, just to check. The weather still looked bad offshore, but passable if I stayed just a little bit inland.

"But don't delay," the last briefer I talked to cautioned. "That inland situation may not hold."

"I'm walking out to the airplane now," I answered. She wished me luck.

I took off and turned the plane southwest. But almost immediately, I found myself looking at a very dark, gray wall in the sky. No matter what Flight Service said, I knew a bad idea when I saw one. The coast looked clear, though, so I headed down the beach and figured I'd just see how far I could get. Within 30 miles, I was flying under a pretty solid overcast, but visibility was good underneath the clouds. I ducked down to about 800 feet off the shoreline to stay clear of Daytona's airspace, and all seemed okay until I got a little further south.

Just south of Daytona is the Kennedy Space Center restricted area, so unless you want to go miles out to sea, you have to cut inland over Titusville. And suddenly, headed inland, things didn't look very good at all. Looking through lowering visibility at lots of gray and rain around me, I called the Daytona controller in a slightly uncertain voice.

"Ummm, Daytona approach, this is niner-four uniform. It looks like I might have some serious weather right in front of me. Are you painting anything there?"

The voice came back, brisk and immediate. "Roger, niner-four-uniform. You have a pretty strong cell, 12 o'clock, 10 miles.

I looked left and right. That cell, it seemed, had friends. "And what about at my 9 o'clock and 3 o'clock?" I inquired.

"Roger, niner-four uniform, you've got cells there, as well.

This was not good. Wherever my plane belonged, it was not here, at 800 feet above the ground in a developing line of weather. Feeling tension creeping into my muscles, I called the controller back.

"Well, Daytona, do you have any advice or ideas? 'Cause short of trying to turn around and go home, I'm fresh out, here."

I could hear the smile in his calm, even voice when he responded.

"Sure, niner-four-uniform. I've got lots of ideas. For starters, why don't you try a one-five-zero degree heading? I'll get you through this."

I turned to the heading. But while that direction was clearer than all the other space around me, it left me looking straight at Kennedy's Vehicle Assembly Building. I keyed the mike again.

"But that's going to take me into the restricted area!" I said with a touch of alarm in my voice. We had dispensed with formal call signs. He knew who was calling him.

The voice of my mother has never been so reassuring as the warm, helpful and calm voice that came back through my headset.

"Hey," my controller said gently. "Don't worry. I'll take care of you."

And he did. He steered me around weather I couldn't have seen through, right down the Shuttle Landing Facility runway, then called ahead and got permission for me to fly right across Patrick Air Force Base, which was the only open spot in the weather at that point. I don't know if he could tell exactly how grateful I was when I thanked him before signing off when I was past the weather, but I hope he could. If it were in my power, I'd give him a special bonus, extra vacation, and my mother would undoubtedly send him Christmas fruitcake for the rest of his life. Because there's nothing so alone as being solo in your airplane when your world is suddenly not okay, and a calm voice reaching out to help you there is the voice of a guardian angel.

I landed in Ft. Lauderdale with a renewed love and appreciation for the extended family in aviation that cares so much about getting all of us home safely. That, in and of itself, is a valuable gift that can come out of having to make our way through the storms of weather, emergency, danger, or hardship … finding that we are not as alone as we imagine, if we muster the humility to reach out and ask for help.

I fueled at Ft. Lauderdale and took off again, bound this time for Key West. The sky was a lovely kind of tropical blue, with clear visibility underneath a scattering of puffy clouds. And I appreciated the beauty and calm all the more because of the thunderstorm nightmare I'd just been through. As I switched over to departure, they cleared me down the coast one mile offshore, and what sounded like "at or below 500 feet." At or below 500 feet? Nobody out where I came from ordered pilots to fly lower than 500 feet above the ground. Surely I'd heard wrong. There must have been a mumbled "thousand" before the 500. That would make more sense. I keyed the mike.

"Was that at or below one-thousand-five hundred feet for niner-four uniform?" I asked. The controller came back sharp and direct.

"Negative, niner-four-uniform. Remain at or below FIVE HUNDRED FEET."

I looked at my altimeter, which was reading about nine hundred feet. I looked down at the water which, truth to tell, didn't look all that far away. Wow. I needed to lose *half* my altitude to comply with the controller's instructions. And while I wasn't going to hit anything over the water, I also wasn't going to make it to an airport from a mile offshore at that altitude, if the engine quit. I took a deep breath and nosed the airplane into an gentle descent. I leveled off around 400 feet, just to give myself some wiggle room, and tried to get used to my new perspective on the world.

It took some getting used to. I kept an eagle eye on the engine instruments all the way past Miami, looking for the slightest change or sign of impending trouble. But as I passed the Miami lighthouse and moved south into the Keys, I began to relax. For one thing, I'd begun to get used to the feel of flying only a few hundred feet above the water. In Africa, pilots talk about the concept of "normalized deviance" to explain how landing on short, unimproved runways half-covered in water can begin to seem "normal" after a while. Do something that pushes your limits for long enough, and it slowly becomes the new benchmark for normal. The boundary for what qualifies as pushing your limits moves further outward. Which, I suppose, says great things about the adaptability of humans, even if it gets us in trouble every now and then.

The other reason I relaxed is because I came to the realization that altitude doesn't actually do you that much good in the Florida Keys. Aside from a couple of airports, there isn't much open land above the water line, and Highway 1 is far too crowded with traffic and wires to make a good landing site. If the engine quit, I was going to land either on a beach or in the water nearby, regardless of whether I was at two hundred feet or two thousand. The thought of ditching was also more palatable because the water was clear, smooth, and relatively shallow. Not to mention reliably warm.

In any event, by the time Miami signed me off to continue my own navigation, I was really beginning to enjoy myself. And with every mile that followed, my fun meter went up another peg. I dropped down to three hundred feet, hoping to see some interesting wildlife in the water below me. The turquoise water was so clear I could see clumps of flora on the sandy bottom and channels of darker green snaking their way out from shore, cut by tiny rivers of water flowing out to the sea.

At that altitude, of course, you really need to keep your wits about you and your focus very clearly on what you're doing. Two or three hundred feet is not the place to go hunting for charts or that stray pen under the seat. Or, for that matter, ruminating about your personal life, the next deadline coming up, or what you should do about that leaky drain in the kitchen.

But there's a huge payoff for being in situations where you're required to focus sharply on where you are to the exclusion of all other concerns. It brings all your senses, and all of your mind's formidable power, to bear on absorbing every detail of the moment you're living, right then. Which means you end up seeing, hearing, feeling, and processing each moment in wide-screen, surround-sound, Technicolor and high-definition detail and clarity. And that, in turn, makes you far more able to feel all the life each one of those moments contains. It's one of the reasons people are drawn to adventure, despite the discomfort it typically entails … and one of the main reasons people say adventure makes them feel so alive.

You also end up noticing all kinds of items that might escape your notice if you weren't so singularly focused. Three hundred feet above the Florida Keys, I became aware, for example, that the water wasn't just one shade of turquoise or blue. It was a seamless montage of every color in the blue/green dictionary; dark blue, light blue, pale turquoise, deep peacock, aquamarine, blue-green, green-blue, emerald and sapphire, with hints of beige in shallow, sandy portions, and streaks of silver where the sun was glinting off its surface.

To my left stretched the stunning expanse of the Florida Straits. To my right were the tree-lined, sandy shores of the Florida Keys. It was like being immersed in a commercial for a tropical island resort, skimming low above the water as picturesque beaches passed in and out of view. I almost had to pinch myself to convince myself it was real ... especially because I'd so recently been in the middle of such a drastically different kind of scene.

To go from one of my darkest encounters with thunderstorm hell to such a blissful immersion in tropical heaven in the span of only a couple of hours was almost too much for my mind to process. None of it seemed real. But I took the same kind of giddy pleasure in my suddenly-idyllic surroundings as someone in the desert might take in a ridiculously tall, cool glass of icy lemonade. For over an hour I skimmed low above the clear island waters, listening to Jimmy Buffett songs through my headset and laughing aloud at the fun and joy of it all, contemplating attitudes, latitudes, and looking for one particular harbor of my own.

A sailor friend of mine, who also happens to have his pilot's license, says that the main difference between flying and sailing is that with flying, you're always trying to get somewhere. In sailing, he says, you already *are* where you want to be.

Most of the time, I'd agree with him. But for that brief stretch of time down the Florida Keys, I was exactly and precisely where I wanted to be: three hundred feet above the water, sailing through an idyllic tropical kingdom that stretched toward a distant, beckoning, and unbroken horizon. I was actually disappointed when I saw Key West appear in the distance.

Without question, the Florida Keys are a beautiful part of the world. And seen from only a couple of hundred feet above the water, skimming along with all my senses on full alert, I was able to drink in all that beauty more intimately, completely and vividly than I would have at a higher altitude. But I think part of the reason that flight stands out in my memory with such enduring brightness is because all that fun and beauty stood in such sharp contrast to the fear and challenge I'd faced only a few hours before. Defy death by thunderstorm and survive to find yourself, in the next moment, immersed in a perfect, tropical paradise of smooth air, clear water, and eye-watering colors and beauty ... and you, too, might find relieved, incredulous laughter bubbling up inside of you. Especially if you had Jimmy Buffett playing in your headset.

Life can turn on a dime and swing from extremes of circumstance and emotion almost faster than we can keep up with, sometimes. Typically, however, we focus more on those times when it goes from good to bad because of some precipitous event. But it can just as easily flip from dark to light. In the dark of a storm, another human can reach out and lend a hand, or shine a light, to show you a safe route home. Or the storm can suddenly abate, shining brilliant sunlight on a scene more beautiful by far because we wondered, for a while there, if we'd ever see sunlight again.

Even now, almost a decade after that flight down the

Florida Keys, I hold the still-razor-sharp memory of that afternoon close in my mind. Not only because of its inherent joy, laughter and beauty, but as a reminder to myself to keep faith in the sunrise, even in the darkest hours of night. The sun also rises. And there is still amazing beauty and endless possibility in the world, just the other side of the storms.

Family Ties
CHAPTER NINE

I don't think that flying is an inherited trait. It may be a desire imprinted in all of our DNA chains, at least as a longing for freedom and a way to break free of the physical bonds that bind us to the earth. Or as a psychological metaphor for a belief in limitless possibility. Almost every three-year-old on the planet, after all, is fascinated with things that fly. They look up, pointing, when an airplane flies by overhead. They want to be spun off the ground. They run down hills, arms outstretched, hoping that one of these times, the wind might actually lift them into the air. Or at least enjoying the fantasy that it might.

What happens to that interest in the years that follow? In some cases, it takes hold with such a fervor that no contrary force can extinguish it. There are some kids who eat, drink, and devour all things aviation from the time that they're little, and who are creatively scheming for ways to get their pilot licenses long before they're old enough to legally hold them.

But in many cases, flight is just one of many interests swirling around in a child's brain. Which of those interests get pursued has as much to do with exposure as it does with DNA. It's no surprise that many children of pilots become pilots. The same links can be found in many other careers, from football and insurance to teaching, medicine, the military, film directing and music. It's hard to imagine careers you've never seen or how you'd become something you've only seen in a movie. But if you have a parent who's doing something daily, it seems attainable. And, in many ways, it *is* more attainable if you have someone to guide you, open doors, teach, encourage and support your forays into the field.

For many children, there's also an undeniable appeal to an activity that allows them to be around, and get attention and approval from, a hero/parent. I know more than a few pilots who began going to the airport as a way to get time with their dads—especially in larger families, where exclusive attention from a parent is a rare and cherished treasure. Sharing an interest in airplanes with a pilot parent can also create a special bond; a secret club between the aviators that the rest of the family doesn't get to share. Perhaps the same is true for golf, sailing, acting, or any number of other hobbies or careers. But not all activities or vocations offer quite the same level of connection.

Flying, for better or worse, is an activity that appeals more to enthusiasts than strict utilitarians. Leaders in the aviation industry have tried for years to get a wider group of people interested in flying their own airplanes. "An airplane in every garage" is a vision and goal that dates back to the early days of the general aviation boom, right after World War II. But the truth remains that, even as we make airplanes easier and more useful to fly (glass and weather in the cockpits, faster speeds, parachutes for safety and smarter airplanes in general), there are only so many people who want to devote the time and resources to becoming a pilot or take on the forces and uncertainty of nature that are always present in the sky.

The people who *are* willing to take on all of that tend to be people who feel some level of passion for the experience and rewards of flight. What inspires that passion? Hard to say, exactly. But flying is inherently more inspirational than many other activities or career tracks. Even with all the modern gadgetry, flight still takes us out of our everyday element and shows us a world that few other humans even get to see, let alone get to know so intimately well. We wrestle with weather, watch a cascading sea of fog tumble over a coastal ridge, take in mountains and ocean from the heights of eagles, and learn the secret geometric art of the farmer, visible only from the air.

Because the consequences for mistakes are so unyielding and final, we also learn tough lessons about ourselves, coming hard up against our fears and working our way through them to strength. And on a few rare occasions in the middle of all that … sometimes when we least expect it … we stumble across something powerfully close to magic in the sky. We may not be able to explain it, but we know we have touched it and known it to be real.

For all of these reasons, and for any number of others that

words can't capture, flight has a special place in the hearts of
those who pursue it. So the pull, and the reward, of sharing such
a heart-felt passion with a parent goes beyond mere approval or
attention. It opens a pathway to secret places in a parent's heart
that all children crave access to, but too few ever find the key
to unlock.

The same is also true in reverse. Parents don't typically
crave understanding from their children. Appreciation, respect
and love, yes. But most parents resign themselves to not being
understood until their children have children of their own. And
even then, it's not a sure bet. But children typically *do* crave
understanding from their parents. The teenage lament, "You
don't understand me!" dates much further back in history than
the airplane. We want our parents to see us for who we truly
are; to grasp why our particular passions are so important to us
and, more importantly, to love and accept whatever they see or
find in us.

In cases where a child's passions conveniently echo those
of a parent, that desire is a lot easier to fulfill. A child of a pilot
doesn't need to work to try to explain to their parent why they
want to fly, or what it brings to their life. Children of non-pilots,
on the other hand—just like parents whose children don't like
flying—have to work a lot harder to bridge that divide.

As it happens, flying does not run in my family. My father
is not a pilot. His father wasn't a pilot. None of my uncles,
great uncles, or any of the other men in the family were pilots.
There have been some pretty impressive women in the mix—
my father's grandmother, for example, had a college degree
(in 1880) and supported her family by raising rabbits.

My mother's mom worked herself through Smith College in defiance of her father and went on to get a master's degree from Harvard before women even got the right to vote. My mother had a career in politics and ran an environmental organization for 23 years, working to clean up the Bronx. But none of them ever went near small airplanes.

When we were kids, my sister Gail always said she wanted to be a pilot—as well as a fireman, a baseball player, an adventurer and an astronaut—but she ended up traveling the world and teaching Spanish, instead. My computer whiz brother David can kick my proverbial tail end in any computerized flight game but, as far as I can tell, never showed any inclination to try out the real McCoy. And even today, the only friends I have who are interested in aviation are pilots I've met since I got my license.

All of those factors may account for why it took me so long to discover that flying was something I enjoyed doing. But it's also meant that my flying has always been a primarily solo endeavor for me, in more ways than one. When I soloed and then passed my private check ride, there was nobody in my world to share the achievements with me. So I just took myself out to dinner to celebrate and noted the events with simple postscripts to my sister, who was in the Peace Corps in Africa at the time.

My flying has been so separate from my family, in fact, that my parents didn't even know I was a pilot for the first eight years I had my license. I do not lie. I didn't purposely hide the fact from them—they knew I spent every weekend at the airport, and that I'd changed careers to become an aviation writer. But for eight years, it seemed that the subject always got mysteriously changed whenever I tried to edge them closer to an idea of what I was doing with all that airport time.

Looking back on it, I can't believe that my dad never pursued the question, even if my mother never did. Looking back on it, he says that he can't, either. But the bottom line is, it wasn't until my first book was published and my mom read the "About the Author" section in the back that my parents discovered that their youngest daughter was a pilot.

My brother thinks it's cool that I fly, and I've gotten the chance to take him flying several times, since we both live on the West Coast. But for years, the only person in my family who seemed truly excited about my flying was my niece, Kinana. The first time I flew my plane to her home in North Carolina, she came bounding into my room every morning to ask if we could go flying that day. When I finally said yes, she cheered and started jumping up and down, pausing only to ask, "Can we go upside down?" When I finally put her in the front seat of the Cheetah, she snapped the headset on her head, grabbed hold of the yoke, and shot me a mischievous sideways look that told me if I ever left the keys in it, she might never bring it back.

Part of the restraint my family exhibits toward my flying may be because they don't share my interest in it. But I think it's also because they worry about me. They almost lost me once, in a car accident, and they know that flying contains risk. And since the reason they know that last item is because I've written about it, I can't dismiss their concerns out of hand. I can only tell them I do my best to be careful, responsible, and safe. But they still worry. Especially my mom.

I understand her perspective much better now than I used to, having watched a niece and two nephews come into the world and become a piece of the family that it would be unthinkable, and unrecoverable, to lose. I still remember the day the intensity of the connection I feel for my niece and nephews, and the enormity of the emotional responsibility I feel for keeping them safe, really hit me. I had taken my sister's kids Kinana and Tyler, who were two and three at the time, to the park. When it came time to leave, I peered over the parked cars at the curb and looked both ways—but evidently not carefully enough. Just as we stepped off the curb, a car shot out of nowhere and zoomed past us, heart-stoppingly close. I yanked Tyler and Kinana back, and they grabbed on to my legs with big, terrified, eyes. Looking down at them, heart racing, I realized that I'd have gladly thrown myself in front of that car to protect or save them. *I'd take a bullet for them.* And there's not a single adult in the world for whom I could promise you I'd do that.

Which is to say, I get a least an echo of the fear parents feel about their children getting hurt. So given that, and given that my mother has never been comfortable with physical risk and adventure (despite working in the South Bronx for over two decades), I came to terms early in my flying career with the fact that I was probably never going to take my parents flying. I thought my dad might actually be intrigued about this flying stuff and want a ride, but I thought he wouldn't want to worry my mom, and the opportunity to test the situation never seemed to present itself.

Until the summer I took my Cheetah to Boston. My mom grew up in Marblehead, Massachusetts, just north of Beantown, and we still spend some time at her childhood home during the summer. I had flown into the Beverly, Massachusetts, airport, which was the nearest I could get to Marblehead ... and also the nearest my Cheetah had ever been to my parents. So one morning, I mentioned to my dad that I'd be happy to take him for a ride, if it was something he thought he'd like to do. His whole face lit up, but before he could answer, my mom cut in.

"Wait a minute," she said sharply.

Uh-oh, I thought as I turned to face her. Here came the objections.

"What about me?" she demanded.

It's amazing how slow the brain can move when it gets completely sideswiped.

"What do you mean, 'what about you?'" I asked.

"I want to go, too," she said.

For the briefest of moments, I wondered if aliens had taken over my mother's body. She couldn't mean it. She didn't like airplanes. She didn't like the fact that I flew them. The sun rose in the east and my mother would never go flying in a small airplane. This is how the universe I knew operated. I stood there for a long moment before I could come up with something resembling a reply.

"You do?" I finally asked. "Why?"

"Because," she answered. "I want to see some of the things you write about for myself."

In any kind of relationship, there are sometimes magical turning-point moments where the lens through which you've seen the other person shifts, showing you a new view of them that forces you to reevaluate who they are and where their limits and edges lie. It's one of the surprises I love best about the complex human animal. No matter how long I've known someone, there's always the possibility of finding new depth, growth, layers and colors that I might never have suspected were there. Indeed, there are probably traits and colors within all of us that even we ourselves don't realize we have until something or someone brings them out of us one day. And in that dawning moment of recognition, new possibilities and beauty suddenly present themselves like the sun rising on a new day.

Perhaps my mother simply had never considered the beauty and perspective that flying might bring until I started writing about it. Or perhaps she simply loves me enough that she wanted to share and understand this piece of my life better, even if it scared her. I think, somehow, it was a combination of both.

In any event, I soon found myself at the Beverly airport, strapping my mom and dad into the Cheetah and praying for smooth air and a well-behaving engine. I took them over the harbor of Marblehead and then up the coast toward Ipswich and back. My dad had a big grin on his face the whole time, and my mom shot an entire roll of film, pointing out landmark after landmark in what sounded like a happy voice from the back seat. When we landed, the grin on my mom's face was every bit as wide as my dad's, and she bubbled on about the flight to my siblings for a week.

A couple of months later, my parents came out to visit me in California. And when I asked my mom what she wanted to do while she was there, going flying was one of the top three things on her wish list. This time, I put her in the front seat, and I took them west out of Santa Rosa, low over the vineyards and across the hills to the coast, where we'd driven the day before. My mom shot another roll of film, tickled by getting to see a landscape she'd toured on the ground from a whole new perspective.

I took them up the coast a bit, past Bodega Bay, toward the Buddhist temple by Fort Ross, keeping a sharp eye on my engine instruments for the slightest hint of change or trouble. Ditching off the cliffs of Northern California is not something you want to do with your parents on board. Or at all, actually. But the engine was as smooth as the autumn evening air. And the view was phenomenal. Redwood forest pushed down to the edges of rocky cliffs that dropped abruptly down to crashing breakers and pinnacle rock formations; shades of green and blue tossed with white foam at the dramatic, wild edge of a continent.

But as we turned back south along the coast, the view my mom had was of the calmer and seemingly endless Pacific, stretching unbroken toward the western horizon. It was the end of the day, and the setting sun had turned the ocean surface a shimmering shade of gold and had painted the sky with brilliant streaks of orange, pink and red. My mom took a few photos and then just sat looking out the window for a long while. Finally, she spoke.

"Oh, Lane, this is beautiful," she said quietly.

My heart turned over, and I thanked whoever it is you thank for those quiet, profound moments when life hands you a gift you know you'll always remember.

"Yeah, mom, it is," I answered.

My parents and I have been through a lot together, over the years. I've almost lost both of them to accident and illness already, and these days I just try to appreciate the gift of whatever days and moments we have. But no matter what the future holds, I will carry the memory of that flight within my heart forever. Fifteen years after getting my license, I finally got to show my mom and dad the world from the sky and see an understanding of that beauty and perspective reflected in their eyes. It's a gift I never thought I'd be able to give them, and a gift I never thought I'd know in return.

It's enough to make one believe in miracles, after all.

The Edges of Space
CHAPTER TEN

Every flight is different, and every flight is special. Pilots comprise less than .002% of the population of the United States, so it's fair to say that few people get to see the particular view and perspective that pilots do from our regular seats, only a few hundred or thousand feet up in the air. But I've also been especially privileged because of my particular line of work. I may not have made a lot of money over the past 20 years, but I've gotten more than my share of extra-special flights — some of which I've talked about in the preceding chapters of this book.

Yet even among all those extra-special flights, there is one that stands out as the most high, the most special, the most once-in-a-lifetime; the one I cannot imagine ever topping. And that was my flight in a U-2 spy plane. Space suit required.

Most pilots would covet the chance to fly a U-2, in part because so few pilots ever have. More people can legitimately wear a Super Bowl championship ring than a solo patch for the U-2, even though the plane has been flying since 1955. But the flight had a particularly special meaning for me because, you see, I never dreamed of being a pilot when I was a kid. I stumbled into aviation when I was 24 years old. But I did once dream of being an astronaut.

I was three years old when I started dreaming of seeing the Earth from space. It was the height of the Mercury/Apollo era, which I'm sure had a lot to do with it. As did the fact that my older sister Gail had decided *she* wanted to be an astronaut, and I pretty much wanted to do whatever she wanted to do. But, still. Girls weren't actually *allowed* to be astronauts back then. But that didn't stop us. Obstacles, even seemingly insurmountable ones, never stopped anyone from dreaming— especially at the age of three.

My father, enlightened soul that he is, even bought my sister and me astronaut outfits for Christmas that year, as encouragement. Well, okay. The flight suit part was actually matching fuzzy sleeper pajamas. But we got white plastic astronaut helmets complete with American flag insignias, moveable Plexiglas visors and even microphones lined with some kind of tissue-like paper to make our voices sound microphone-funny when we talked through them. Of all the photos my parents took of us as kids, the one that's my absolute favorite—so much so that I stole it out of the family album one year, had copies made, and now have it sitting on my desk— is the photo of Gail and me, that Christmas morning, trying out our new space suits in the front hallway.

Even now, more than a generation later, I can almost hear the gleeful laughter pealing out of the photo from my giggling, happy face. I remember feeling that way. It's the same look I must have had on my face when, about that same age, I used to stand on hilltops on breezy days, head thrown back and arms stretched out, trying to drink the wind. Three-year-olds may not know a lot about finance, science, or history, but they know joy better than any adult I know. Joy, laughter, and how to be completely and deliriously immersed in a moment. They also know how to dream.

But time passed, and life moved on. I got more interested in drama, arts and writing, and the dream of space travel faded. Yet I never forgot that plastic space helmet, or the dream that had gone with it. And while my path went in a very different direction, the dream never really died. So, okay. I wasn't ever going to be an astronaut. But just once, I thought ... just once ... wouldn't it be cool to go far enough off the planet to have to wear a space suit? And far enough ... maybe not all the way to Space, but far enough to see the curvature of the Earth? That would be enough. More than enough.

It was still a pie-in-the-sky kind of dream, of course. But when I met a U-2 pilot named John Cabigas at a Cub fly-in a few years ago (turns out a lot of U-2 pilots fly little tailwheel airplanes in their spare time), and he suggested that I might be able to get a ride in a U-2 for an article, it all came rushing back.

As it turns out, however, getting approval to fly in a U-2 is a very, very difficult thing to accomplish, even if you *are* an aviation writer. In the end, it took two and half years of effort to get the flight approved. And even then, it was only because the pilots within the U-2 squadron took up the cause.

The U-2, you see, is more than just a high-profile reconnaissance airplane. It's also the only tailwheel aircraft still in the Air Force inventory. It may not be a *conventional* tailwheel, because when the U-2 was built, jet engines weren't very powerful. So for the U-2 to reach its design altitudes of 60,000 feet and above, it had to be incredibly lightweight. Everything that wasn't absolutely essential was jettisoned. Including, for the first few years, an ejection seat.

To save additional weight, the U-2 was also designed with only two landing gear (instead of a normal airplane's three), arranged one behind the other along the centerline of the fuselage. Portable wheels are put under the wings for taxi and take off, but they drop away as soon as the plane leaves the ground. So when the U-2 comes in to land, it is, as one pilot put it, "like landing a bicycle on a runway." A *tailwheel* bicycle, at that.

That unique configuration makes the U-2 the most difficult aircraft in the Air Force inventory to land. And that, in turn, means that it takes a very special kind of pilot to want to fly the "Dragon Lady," as the U-2 is nicknamed. It takes a pilot who loves flying stick and rudder (because the U-2 has completely unboosted, cable controls); a pilot who doesn't mind taking on a landing experience that is harder than more modern planes offer and which, like golf, can never be mastered to perfection; a pilot who doesn't mind being humbled every now and then, because the beauty of the art

when you get it right is so sweet; and a pilot who takes pride in
flying a plane that's not the newest on the block but has a long
and significant history.

A pilot, in other words, who loves old tailwheel
flying machines.

Why is that relevant? Because there's a kind of kinship among pilots who love old traildraggers. I'd never flown
a U-2. But I'd flown and written about other tailwheel airplanes
I had known and loved, including my old 1946 Cessna 120.
And apparently, a number of the squadron pilots had read
enough of those stories to feel, quite strongly, that I would
understand, and might be able to put into words for them, why
the U-2 was so special and why they loved flying her. Even
when she humbled them.

I never dreamed, when I bought into my Cessna 120, with
its leaky brakes, five instruments, 100 mph cruise speed, and
finicky spring gear and tailwheel, that it would be my ticket to
Space. But in the end, the reason I found myself in my Cheetah
one November day, en route to Beale AFB to actually fly
a U-2 with Maj. John "Cabi" Cabigas, space suit and all, wasn't
because of anything I did directly to make that dream happen.
It was because, in the course of simply doing what I love most,
I'd connected with some distant but kindred spirits out there.
Kindred spirits who just happened to fly an airplane that
required space suits and flew high enough to see the curvature
of the Earth.

There's a lesson in that, somewhere.

Cabi arranged for me to get permission to land my
Cheetah at Beale, itself, and Luke "Loco" Locowich, another

squadron pilot, arranged for the Cheetah to have its own hangar while it was there. I stepped back after parking the Cheetah in its cavernous, U-2 hangar, a huge American flag hanging from the center beam right above it, and smiled.

"Don't you ever say mom never took you anywhere cool," I admonished the Cheetah before closing the hangar door.

But what touched me most was the welcome packet Luke gave me upon landing. It consisted of a hand-made leather chart bag for my airplane, filled with two water bottles, a couple of pens, and a folder with base maps and information. On top of the maps was a typewritten page with several poetic quotes about flight, and high flight in particular. And at the bottom of the page was a hand-written note that said, simply, "Please let us know how we can be of assistance. We're so glad you're here."

It's one of the things that never ceases to amaze me about flying. In the most unexpected moments and corners of the world, you land your airplane, thinking you're very far from home. And then you talk to a fellow pilot there, get a welcome note, or recognize a kindred spirit in the face of a stranger, and you realize that you're not so far from home, at all.

The next day, I discovered why so few people ever get U-2 flights approved: training and preparing for a U-2 flight is a three-day process that takes a truly staggering amount of staff time, energy, focus, and expense. Unlike flights that operate at lower altitudes, anyone in a U-2 has to be prepared to survive in what is, essentially, an unsurvivable environment … in a plane that is almost completely manual, with two completely separate cockpits. (U-2s are single-seat airplanes, but five were modified into two-cockpit versions for training purposes. Those planes are the only ones you can get a ride in.) In the case of an emergency, the pilot can't eject or help the back-seater in the U-2, and ejecting from a U-2 at 70,000 feet with 150 extra pounds of space suit and gear is a very serious matter.

As a result, I spent the next two and half days trying desperately to absorb and learn not only normal operation of a space suit and the U-2 cockpit, but also a long list of emergency and survival procedures and mancuvers. I learned how to disconnect myself from all the life support and safety systems in the U-2 cockpit if we crash landed or landed away from an airport—10 separate hoses and clamps and cotter-pinned connections that I was supposed to be able to undo in less than 60 seconds—in space gloves, no less. I learned about the plane's manual ejection procedures that would leave me attached to the seat, hurtling through thin air at high speed, with a raft of tasks ahead of me if I wanted to hit the ground alive and uninjured.

At 15,000 feet, the seat would drop away and main chute would deploy. I'd then have to check the canopy, untangling inverted or split lobes as necessary and cutting away no more than six lines with the knife I'd be carrying in my suit pocket. I'd have to reach up and yank the control lines free so I could steer. I'd have to close valves and disconnect my seat kit of survival gear from my body so its weight wouldn't break my back on landing. (A long lanyard would keep that, and my personal life raft (no kidding) attached to me, but would allow them to hit the ground first.) I made notes to steer away from objects and into the wind while kicking off my ejection seat spurs and disconnecting my oxygen hoses and unlocking my

helmet visor. Then I'd have to remember to keep my knees and
feet together, look straight ahead, and prepare to land hard.

After learning and practicing all those maneuvers in
various simulators, I then learned some basics of survival.
I learned that body temperature is paramount to protect; food,
shelter, and even water can wait a day or more. Help might
arrive by then. I learned how to tie a tourniquet, fire flares,
repair a life raft, desalinize water, start a fire with a magnesium
stick, signal with a mirror, flares, or water dye, operate a military
ELT and radio, and even what berries and insects are edible.
(A waterproof guide is included in the survival kit).

After all that, I learned how to live in a space suit—how
to keep air flowing through it, because otherwise body
temperature rises one degree every six minutes and at 107
degrees you die; how to use the pressurized relief system; how
to eat tubes of food mush and drink through a straw that could
be slid through the helmet housing, and how to recognize
potential signs of trouble.

The space suit is necessary, because at altitudes above
63,000 feet—a point known as "Armstrong's Line"—the air
pressure is so low that the boiling point of liquid becomes a
mere 98.6 degrees. So without a suit to keep the pressure of
your body below that point, your blood would boil. The U-2
cockpit is pressurized, but only to 29,500 feet—which led one
pilot to tell me that flying the U-2 was like being "encased
in rubber, sitting in a telephone booth, on top of Mt. Everest."
But there are other potential problems at altitudes that high:
hypoxia, "the bends," and other physiological discomforts
and dangers.

Some people also aren't cut out for the claustrophobic world of a space suit. So half a day was devoted to a practice run in an altitude chamber, including explosive and slow decompressions that tested my ability to handle an emergency in a fully-inflated space suit. As it turns out, my arms are too short, in full Michelin-Man deployment mode, to reach the U-2's ejection handle. Which was good to know ahead of time. For me, the only ejection option would be the back-up system, activated by opening a cover to the left of the seat, fumbling for the T-handle inside of it (in space gloves, mind you), and pulling the T-handle while also pulling my arms close to my body so they wouldn't get cut off in the course of departing the airplane.

Only after all of that training and testing—which required the full attention of a team of military personnel for two full days—did we get to the more normal preparation for a flight: a cockpit check-out and mission briefing.

The morning of the flight, I was up early for a pre-flight breakfast of mild eggs and toast and a quick briefing on weather and the mission profile. Then Cabi and I went to get suited up. A team of two to four people is required to suit up a U-2 pilot. The suits are so tight you can't even get in or out of them unassisted, and each connection has to be checked and double-checked, since any flaw or breach could prove fatal. Then, once the layers of inner socks, outer socks, inner gloves, outer gloves, boots, vest, and helmet are assembled, the helmet visor is closed and locked. The world and all its noise is now a distant, muffled reality outside of your cocoon, and it will remain so until after you land.

The dominant noise now becomes your own breathing—

the raspy sound of oxygen being drawn in and your breath exhaling through a system that sounds exactly like the one used by Darth Vader in the movie *Star Wars*. But the regular rhythm of inhaling and exhaling, against the sharply muffled external world, is strangely soothing. You can't communicate without a lot of effort, so you let go of trying. The world will take care of itself. Your only job now is to breathe. All else drops away. Breathe, relax, and focus on the mission ahead. As I waited the required hour needed to clear the nitrogen from my body before take off, I even closed my eyes for a bit.

Surprisingly soon, someone was touching me on my sleeve, and there were two airmen at my sides, ready to help me out of the recliner where I'd been sitting, astronaut-style, and into the van that would take us to the plane. It was time to go. One of the airmen carried the small, portable oxygen "suitcase" that I'd seen so many times from X-15 and astronaut films; my survival system until I was hooked into the one in the airplane itself.

We arrived at the plane and shook the hands of the ground crew—a tradition among pilots who know just how much their lives depend on the work the crew around them does. "Never in my Air Force career, before coming to the U-2, did I feel like my life was in the hands of my support crew," one pilot told me. "But here, the environment we operate in is so deadly, they know that if they so much as attach a glove wrong, you're going to die."

Another airman strapped me in and attached me to all the safety and life support systems in the cockpit. Final checks, thumbs-up on communication and breathing systems, a reminder to pull the three safety pins on my ejection seat when we were on the runway just before take off, and the canopy was closed and locked over my head. I was now very close to committed. I was really going to do this. Go far enough off the planet that the environment alone would kill me if anything went wrong. What the hell was I thinking?

Cabi's cockpit was ahead and below mine, so I couldn't even see him. All I could see was the black top of his cockpit, blending into the fuselage stretching out in front of me. We were still on the ground, but I was now far more a creature of space; already dependent on my artificial breathing and cooling systems for survival. From this point forward, if something went wrong, I might very well have to use some of that information I'd crammed into my brain to get myself out of it. And as I looked around the cockpit, with its "do not touch" rocket motors to blow the canopy, the "bailout" light on the panel, and all its antiquated switches, knobs and systems it began to sink in just how bad a bad day in a U-2 could be.

Why, exactly, had I wanted to do this so badly?

Fortunately, we were cleared to start, and Cabi's voice came over the intercom with taxi instructions, leaving no room for other thoughts or doubts. Sometimes, it's good not to have too much time to think about an adventure ahead of time. Especially right before you leap.

The ground steering of a U-2 is actually quite similar to that of a Cheetah, so taxiing was simpler than I'd expected. We pulled onto the runway, and our chase pilot, Lt. Col. Jon "Huggy" Huggins, pulled up beside us to check that all was well and we both had our safety pins out of the ejection seats and were ready to go.

Chase pilots, in the U-2 world, don't fly aircraft. They drive sports cars. This is because the long nose and wings of a U-2 severely restrict a pilot's visibility on takeoff and landing. So a chase pilot drives down the runway in close formation behind the U-2 to alert the pilot to any deviations or problems. On landing, the chase pilot actually talks the pilot down, calling out altitude and any right/left course corrections as the U-2 approaches its flare and touchdown. One of the dichotomies of being a U-2 pilot is that you are once more alone, in a single-seat, single-ship formation high up in the stratosphere, and also more dependent on other support personnel, than almost any other pilot in the world.

All checks completed, we were cleared for takeoff, and Cabi talked me through a steady application of power as we started to roll. The whole point of the U-2's configuration and construction is to get an incredibly high thrust to weight ratio. Which means that at full power, the U-2 accelerates with a serious kick. And while it doesn't do vertical rolls to 15,000 feet, like an F-16 might, the U-2 can go from sea level to 62,000 feet in 20 minutes. And then stay up there, un-refueled, for more than 12 hours.

On our flight, however, we leveled off at 10,000 feet first, because Cabi wanted to show me how challenging the U-2 was to fly in the thick air of the lower altitudes. At 10,000 feet and 90 knots, a U-2 takes 60 pounds of force to roll the yoke over, and 150 pounds of force to push the rudder pedals to the floor. But still, the plane handled much like other solid, rudder-heavy airplanes I'd flown, like the DC-3. At 130 knots, however, that started to change. It was a real challenge to get enough rudder and aileron movement to get a 30-degree bank accomplished. And at 220 knots, the task was all but impossible. I put two hands on the yoke and turned, *hard.* No luck. I had my full body force leaning into the yoke before I got it to move.

But there's also a reason the U-2 is referred to as a Lady as well as a Dragon. Because when we climbed up to 62,000 feet and leveled off at cruise speed (about .71 Mach), the U-2 turned into the smoothest-handling sports car you'd ever want to fly. She was a delight of harmonized grace, with finger-touch controls. The Dragon Lady is a plane that's very clear about where she wants to be. And she gets grouchy and cantankerous if you try to fly her anywhere else.

"You either wrestle with the dragon or dance with the lady," Cabi told me. "And you're never quite sure which one she's going to be."

From that point, we engaged the autopilot and eased our way higher. The autopilot is important in a U-2, because there are points above 62,000 feet where a mere 10 knots stands in between the plane's stall speed and redline—the infamous "coffin corner." And, as the name implies, straying either side of that narrow window tends to end the same way: badly.

As the autopilot edged us into the higher reaches of the atmosphere, I was also able to pay a little more attention to our surroundings. And what I saw left me speechless with an almost reverent sense of wonder.

Frost was beginning to accumulate inside the windows of my cockpit, so I reached a gloved hand up and scraped a clear opening in the ice. The long, graceful lines of the left wing extended almost 50 feet into the impossibly thin air surrounding us. Normally when I fly, I'm off the surface of the planet, but still deep within the ocean of air that cushions and protects us from the vast and icy universe beyond. But in the U-2, even the majority of that atmospheric ocean lay beneath me. I wasn't so much flying *in* it as I was surfing just beneath its surface.

I looked out along the long, dark wing of the U-2. If I'd leaned closer to the window—no mean feat in a cumbersome space suit and helmet—I probably could have looked down and identified some of the individual landmarks below. But at that moment, my focus was not local, but global. I glanced at the altimeter. We were well over 70,000 feet, and my world was bigger than it'd ever been. Ocean and mountains were contained in a single glance; the California coastline seemed to rise in front of us as we made our way south, even as the land and sea dropped away to either side. The curve of the Earth was only faintly discernable, even at that altitude. But it was there, a multi-hued, bending arc of horizon that belied the foolish notion that any place on Earth was flat.

Ringing the brown-and-blue hues of the planet's surface was a narrow band of white haze. Our atmosphere. And even though there was still a long distance between us and the formal boundary of Space, the U-2's wing seemed to be skimming along the top of that precious atmospheric haze. Above the haze, there was a thin line of light blue, where enough water molecules still existed to create the illusion of color. Above that, the sky got progressively darker, from midnight blue to black.

I looked left, then right, and finally just sat quietly, in awe of the planet I call home. It's such a complex place—at once a vast and powerful rock spinning slowly through the cosmos, and also a unique and delicate ecosystem sustained by an impossibly fragile cushion of air. As I got a taste of how hostile, cold and dark the cosmos was, lurking just outside that fragile protective bubble, it suddenly seemed very important to me that we take very good care of that fragile ecosystem. An ecosystem, I reminded myself, that I had left in order to purchase this view.

We don't belong here.

Somewhere in the back recesses of my brain, I couldn't escape the feeling that Cabi and I were surreptitious infiltrators—rebels who'd cunningly figured out a way to slip out of our world into the forbidden edges of another, where only creatures who didn't need oxygen, air pressure or heat could survive. Isn't this what led Icarus to his doom?

But I was also aware that this was the view I'd dreamed about ever since I was a little girl. I was high above the planet, in a space suit, gazing out at the curvature of the Earth. I never thought I'd get to experience this even once, and it was highly unlikely that I'd ever get back here again.

"Remember this moment," I whispered fiercely to myself, as if the statement itself could, by sheer force of will, burn all the impressions and sensations of the moment indelibly on my mind's memory banks.

All too soon, it was time to start back. We started descending and kicked the autopilot off at about 50,000 feet. Cabi planned to shoot a few touch and go's, even though it was gusting 12–15 knots across the runway at Beale (the top crosswind generally allowed for the U-2 is 15 knots), and he asked me to follow through with him on our first landing. So as we banked around from our initial approach over the field and circled onto final, I put my gloved hands on the yoke and my booted feet on the rudder pedals and valiantly tried to keep up with Cabi as he wrestled the plane down final.

I didn't keep up long. Within a few seconds, I jerked my hands and feet as far back from the controls as I could get them. I've seen pilots wrestle a tailwheel down onto the runway in windy conditions many times. I've done it a few times myself. But this gave "wrestle" a whole new level of meaning. It was as if the controls were possessed; jumping apoplectically through more rapid contortions and combinations of full-stop deflections in all axes than I've ever seen a pilot manage. Cabi's words came back to me: "You either wrestle with the dragon, or dance with the lady." Wrestle was right.

When we finally came to a full stop on our third landing, I had a whole new level of respect for the tailwheel talent that U-2 pilots possess. As well as for the effort they go to—not just to fly this amazing, challenging aircraft, but for each other, as well.

One of the ironies of my U-2 flight, in fact, was that in all my years of dreaming about seeing the curve of the Earth and wearing a real-life space suit, it was a solitary vision; a thing I wanted for myself, alone. But in the time I spent with the U-2 squadron and all the training and ground personnel who worked so hard to make sure I got through the experience in one piece, the last thing I felt was alone. For there is a sense of community among the U-2 pilots and crews that goes beyond simple loyalty to the corps or mission.

In part, I think the bond comes from the uniqueness of the mission and the small number of pilots who've ever joined the club. It may also reflect the fact that every U-2 pilot is there because he or she passionately wants to be there. Another factor is undoubtedly the unusual level of interdependence among U-2 pilots and their crews, and the fact that they deploy in very small groups for weeks or months at a time.

But somewhere in the mix is also something else: a shared love of flying for the pure joy of flying, and a shared love for the same remarkable but challenging lady. I don't pretend to truly understand. I haven't wrestled the Dragon to the ground, or spent long, solitary nights on patrol high above the Earth, over hostile territory, with only the mission and the stars to keep me company.

But I do know something about loving an old tailwheel airplane that isn't always easy or forgiving. And I suspect that part of the passion pilots feel for the legendary Dragon Lady stems from the fact that, unlike more technologically advanced and automated military jets, flying the U-2 is *personal.* To fly the U-2 is to get to know the actual feel of its cables and control surfaces. To judge its alignment by a yaw string. To learn to intuitively sense any side-forces on landing. We may dream about many new and shiny things, but we love best those things we know well—unvarnished, unfiltered, and through touch, sense, and memorable shared experience.

In the early days of aviation, even fighter pilots had that kind of nuanced feel for their airplanes. They had to. But in today's world of computerized flight systems, the U-2 offers Air Force pilots a rare opportunity to combine the romance of stick-and-rudder flying with the best technological know-how—not only in life-support systems, but in cutting edge reconnaissance equipment that imbues every flight with a sense of meaningful accomplishment and purpose.

Fifty years after it took to the skies, the U-2 is still a study in opposites. So was my flight. High above the Earth, I was alone with my thoughts, my senses, my writing board, and my tubes of water and gushy apple pie. But I've never felt so acutely aware of my reliance on others as I did in that space suit, gazing at the top edges of the atmosphere. As well as how lonely the sky would be if we didn't have anyone waiting to welcome us back home again.

Fortunately, I had nothing to worry about, on that front. When Cabi and I pulled up in front of base headquarters, I looked out and saw a dozen or more squadron pilots waiting to welcome me back with cheers of goodwill. And when I look at the photos they took of me, in those precious moments of return, I see the same kind of unrestrained joy as another camera captured, one long ago Christmas morning.

It really *happened.* That's pretty amazing, in and of itself. But the joy on my face isn't just about the space suit, or even about seeing the curvature of the Earth. It's about the family that made it happen, and who were then waiting to welcome me home at the end of the adventure.

Was it all that I ever dreamed it would be? Oh, yeah. All that and so very, very much more.

epilogue

Picking a favorite flight is a little like picking a favorite child. All of my flights have been different, and all of them have been special in one way or another. The mere act of leaving the earth just because you want to is special, so anything that happens after that is, in many ways, just icing on the cake. I also have many more cherished memories from my two decades of flying than I could fit in this collection.

I chose these particular stories because they spoke to some of the best parts of flying: the distant and exotic places it can take you, the people it can allow you to meet and connect with, the astounding natural beauty it shows you in some of the more inaccessible corners of the earth and sky, and the adventures it allows you to have.

But flying isn't just about physical rewards of excitement or beauty. It's also a profound teacher of important internal lessons about life, being human, and what matters most in how we go through our time on this planet. It reminds us that magic can be found anywhere, even in everyday and unexpected moments and places. It shows us how important the connections we share with our families and communities are ... both for our hearts, and for our survival. It reminds us that perspective is everything, and that there's no obstacle we can't rise above. It teaches us not to give up when the going gets rough, and that we're really a lot stronger than we might have imagined we were. It helps us learn to respect our limitations and build on our strengths. It forces us to be honest with ourselves. It shows us that anything is possible. And it also reminds us of what joy and life feel like when they wash over you in visceral, three-dimensional waves of sensation and emotion.

The stories I chose to include here speak to some of those gifts, as well.

The flights in this collection are some of the treasured memories I will pull out on the rainy days of my life. And when I do, I will smile again at the laughter, beauty, magic and life that still bubble forth from them, even from the worn pages of my past. But one of the most important lessons that flying teaches is the importance of moving forward. If an airplane helps to pull us out of our narrow vision and funky blues, at least part of the reason is because flying forces us to *keep moving*. Airplanes don't fly backwards, and they don't fly at all if they stand still. They are creatures of the future—always heading somewhere new, seeking out a new horizon or destination from which they will set out again for yet another peak or coast.

Humans are not so limited in their design, of course. We can, if we choose, spend most of our time looking back. We just don't gain a whole lot of happiness that way.

Most animals don't have an intellectual understanding of the future. They don't worry about retirement accounts, their parents dying, whether their job will still be there next year, or even if they really should have tried to go pro, back when they had the chance. Which is why animals can be completely happy in the moment.

There's some wisdom in that approach, of course—I've long said that the key to feeling completely alive isn't to live as if each moment is your last, but to live as if to make each moment last forever. The more we focus on the moment we're living, right now, the more we're able to drink in all the life that moment contains.

But because humans can envision the future beyond the present, much of our happiness is tied to what we see there. It's hard to be completely happy in the moment if you think everything that follows will be sad.

So even as I look back and cherish what has been, and try my best to be present in the moment I'm living right now … I also know that the secret to a vibrant life is to keep seeking out new learning, new horizons, and new moments of laughter and joy. It's been an amazing, wonderful, and unforgettable ride. But the best part of the party is always the part that isn't over yet. So of all the flights I've ever had, from serene to dramatic, from low-level Cub flying to high-altitude space suits, my answer as to which one is my favorite is actually quite simple.

It's the next one.

acknowledgments

There are any number of parallel universes in which this book would never have been written. Where I didn't become a pilot, or a writer, or didn't go to work at *Flying* magazine, or didn't have all these flights, or didn't get the idea of compiling them, or didn't get the support I needed to create the finished product you see here.

For this book to exist, a lot of stars had to line up. Which had less to do with cosmic coincidence than it did some very, very, very good friends who helped to put those stars in motion. There was my friend George, who sent me a book of short stories about flying and gave me the idea of getting a biplane ride half a lifetime ago. Without that, there wouldn't have been anything else. There was my friend Jim, who not only made the purchase and upkeep of the Cessna 120 possible and shared a lot of flying adventures with me, but who also convinced me

I needed to quit my corporate job and become a writer. Without that, the stories never would have been told.

There was my dear friend Pat, who not only got me my *Flying* job, but who also has been a brilliant brainstorming partner, editing whiz, marketing magician and stalwart friend, in good times and bad, for almost 20 years. This book was her idea, and much of the content bears her editing fingerprints. And finally, there is Ed, who is cooking dinner even as we speak, so I can work on this project ... like he has almost every night for the past few weeks. It's not easy to be around a writer on deadline, especially when the words aren't cooperating. And I am grateful beyond words for his love, laughter, patience and support. Like I've often said ... a good traveling companion makes all the difference in the journey.

I also have to thank all the *Flying* magazine readers over the years who not only read my column, but sent notes back sharing their own unforgettable moments, stories, and reactions to my work. If you had not offered my words such a warm and welcoming home in your lives, it would have been a very short ride.